COOKING
FOR THE FAMILY

Edited by Norma MacMillan and Wendy James
Home economist Gilly Cubitt

ORBIS PUBLISHING London

Introduction

By buying carefully – selecting foods that are in season – and
making the best use of ingredients, a cook on a budget can
produce tempting, satisfying meals for the family. There
are lots of ideas in this book for appetising, economical
dishes that will suit any occasion.

Both imperial and metric measures are given for each recipe;
you should follow only one set of measures as they are not
direct conversions. All spoon measures are level unless
otherwise stated. Pastry quantities are based on the amount
of flour used. Dried herbs may be substituted for fresh
herbs: use one-third of the quantity.

Photographs were supplied by Editions Atlas, Editions Atlas/Cedus,
Editions Atlas/Masson, Editions Atlas/Zadora, Archivio IGDA, Lavinia
Press Agency, Orbis GmbH, Wales Tourist Board

The material in this book has previously appeared in *The Complete Cook* and *Cooking on a Budget*

First published 1985 in Great Britain by Orbis Publishing Limited,
20-22 Bedfordbury, London WC2

©EDIPEM, Novara 1976
©1978, 1979, 1980, 1981, 1984, 1985 Orbis Publishing, London

ISBN 0-85613-816-9
Printed in Italy

Contents

Portuguese vegetable soup

Overall timing 1½ hours plus soaking

Freezing Not suitable

To serve 6

4 oz	Dried haricot beans	125 g
3 pints	Chicken stock	1.7 litres
2	Large onions	2
6 tbsp	Oil	6x15 ml
12 oz	Waxy potatoes	350 g
3	Garlic cloves	3
1 lb	Spinach	450 g
	Salt and pepper	
4	Thick slices of bread	4

Put the beans in large saucepan and cover with cold water. Bring to the boil and boil for 2 minutes. Remove from heat, cover and leave to soak for 2 hours.

Drain beans and return to pan. Add stock, bring to the boil, cover and simmer for about 1 hour till tender.

Meanwhile, peel and chop the onions. Heat 2 tbsp (2x15 ml) oil in a saucepan, add the onions and fry till transparent. Peel and dice the potatoes. Peel and crush garlic. Add potatoes and garlic to pan and fry, stirring, for 5 minutes. Add pan contents to the beans and simmer for 5 minutes.

Shred the spinach. Add to the pan with seasoning and simmer for 5 minutes.

Remove the crusts from the bread and cut into cubes. Heat remaining oil in a frying pan, add the bread and fry till golden. Drain croûtons on kitchen paper.

Taste soup and adjust seasoning. Pour into a warmed tureen. Sprinkle with croûtons and serve immediately.

Pea and bacon soup

Overall timing 2¾ hours plus overnight soaking

Freezing Suitable

To serve 6

12 oz	Dried whole green peas	350 g
4 pints	Water	2.3 litres
2 lb	Knuckle of smoked bacon	900 g
	Salt and pepper	

Put peas in a saucepan and cover with the cold water. Leave to soak overnight.

Add the bacon knuckle to the pan and bring to the boil. Skim off any scum. Cover and simmer for 1½–2 hours till the bacon and peas are tender.

Remove and drain the bacon joint. Discard the skin and bone and cut the meat into small cubes. Reserve one third of the peas. Purée the remaining peas in a blender or by pressing through a sieve. Return the puréed peas and reserved whole peas to the saucepan. Bring to the boil, stirring occasionally.

Add the diced bacon, and season to taste. Pour into a warmed tureen and serve with crispbread.

Provençal cod soup

Overall timing 1 hour

Freezing Not suitable

To serve 4

1	Large onion	1
1	Leek	1
1	Large tomato	1
2 tbsp	Oil	2x15 ml
1	Stalk of fresh fennel (optional)	1
2	Garlic cloves	2
2½ pints	Water	1.5 litres
	Bouquet garni	
	Orange rind	
¼ teasp	Saffron	1.25 ml
	Salt and pepper	
1¾ lb	Potatoes	750 g
1 lb	Cod fillets	450 g
4	Thick slices of bread	4
1 tbsp	Chopped parsley	15 ml

Peel and slice onion. Trim and finely chop leek. Blanch, peel and chop tomato. Heat oil in a large saucepan. Add onion, leek and tomato and cook, stirring, for 5 minutes.

Chop fennel, if using. Peel and crush garlic. Add water, bouquet garni, fennel, a strip of orange rind, garlic, saffron and pepper. Bring to the boil.

Peel and thickly slice potatoes. Add to pan and cook for 10 minutes. Chop cod fillets into pieces and add with seasoning. Cook for a further 15 minutes.

Remove cod and potatoes with a draining spoon and place in warmed serving dish. Put the slices of bread in a warmed soup tureen and pour the cooking juices over. Sprinkle with parsley. Serve soup and cod together or as separate courses.

Rice and offal soup

Overall timing 2¼ hours

Freezing Not suitable

To serve 4

1 lb	Calves' lights	450 g
1	Calf's heart	1
8 oz	Calf's liver	225 g
1	Large onion	1
4 pints	Stock or water	2.2 litres
	Salt and pepper	
3 oz	Long grain rice	75 g
2	Eggs	2
3 tbsp	Orange juice	3x15 ml
2 tbsp	Chopped parsley	2x15 ml

Trim the lights, heart and liver. Cut into small chunks. Peel and finely chop the onion. Place all in a large saucepan and add the stock or water and seasoning. Bring to the boil, skim the surface and cover. Reduce heat and simmer for 1¾ hours till meat is tender.

Stir in the rice and simmer for a further 15 minutes, stirring frequently.

Beat the eggs and orange juice together in a bowl. Gradually add two ladles of the cooking liquor, stirring constantly. Pour the mixture into the soup and cook for 5 minutes without boiling. Add parsley, taste and adjust seasoning and serve immediately.

Chicken noodle soup

Overall timing 10 minutes

Freezing Not suitable

To serve 4

2½ pints	Chicken stock	1.5 litres
3 oz	Fine egg noodles	75 g
2 tbsp	Lemon juice	2x15 ml
	Salt and pepper	
2 tbsp	Chopped parsley	2x15 ml

Put the stock into a large saucepan. Bring to the boil and add the noodles. Boil for 3–4 minutes till tender.

Add the lemon juice and seasoning and sprinkle with chopped parsley. Serve with a side dish of grated mature Cheddar cheese.

Bacon dumpling soup

Overall timing 2¾ hours

Freezing Suitable: add dumplings to stock after thawing

To serve 4

12 oz	Stale white bread	350 g
½ pint	Milk	300 ml
2 oz	Lean bacon rashers	50 g
1 oz	Butter	25 g
1	Onion	1
1	Garlic clove	1
1 tbsp	Chopped parsley	15 ml
¼ teasp	Dried marjoram	1.25 ml
	Salt and pepper	
3	Eggs	3
4 oz	Self-raising flour	125 g
2 pints	Stock	1.1 litres

Remove crusts from bread, then soak in milk for 2 hours. Derind and chop bacon. Fry in butter till crisp.

Peel and finely chop onion. Peel and crush garlic. Put both into bowl with bread, bacon, parsley and marjoram. Season and add eggs. Mix together well. Sift in flour and stir until absorbed.

Heat the stock in a large saucepan. Make the bacon mixture into 1 inch (2.5 cm) balls and roll them in a little flour so they don't fall apart when cooking. Add the dumplings to the stock and simmer for 15 minutes. Serve hot.

Spicy bortsch

Overall timing 2½ hours

Freezing Suitable

To serve 6

1	Carrot	1
1 lb	Parsnips	450 g
4	Tomatoes	4
1	Onion	1
9	Cloves	9
1 lb	Beef bones	450 g
1 lb	Stewing beef	450 g
½ teasp	Salt	2.5 ml
1 teasp	Sugar	5 ml
6	Peppercorns	6
1	Bay leaf	1
2½ pints	Cold water	1.5 litres
1½ lb	Raw beetroots	700 g
4 oz	Red or green cabbage	125 g

Peel and chop carrot and parsnips. Chop tomatoes. Peel onion and spike with cloves. Crack bones; dice beef.

Put vegetables, bones and beef into a large saucepan with salt, sugar, peppercorns, bay leaf and water. Bring to the boil, cover and simmer for 2 hours or until meat is tender. Remove bones, onion and bay leaf.

Peel and coarsely grate beetroots. Chop cabbage. Add to pan and simmer, uncovered, for a further 12–15 minutes.

Florentine minestrone

Overall timing 2¾ hours plus soaking

Freezing Suitable: add cabbage and macaroni after reheating

To serve 4

8 oz	Dried haricot beans	225 g
2	Large carrots	2
2	Stalks of celery	2
1	Garlic clove	1
2	Onions	2
4 tbsp	Oil	4x15 ml
1½ teasp	Dried mixed herbs	7.5 ml
14 oz	Can of tomatoes	397 g
8 oz	Cabbage	225 g
4 oz	Short macaroni	125 g
	Salt and pepper	

Place beans in large saucepan and cover with cold water. Bring to the boil and boil for 2 minutes. Remove from heat, cover and soak for 2 hours.

Drain beans, return to pan, cover with boiling water and simmer for 2 hours.

Peel and chop carrots; chop celery. Peel and crush garlic. Peel and slice onions. In a large saucepan, heat oil and fry vegetables until golden.

Drain beans, reserving cooking liquor. Purée half the beans. Add beans, whole and puréed, to fried vegetables with cooking liquor, herbs and tomatoes. Bring to the boil. Shred cabbage and add to boiling soup with macaroni and seasoning. Simmer for 20 minutes.

Rice and cabbage soup

Overall timing 45 minutes

Freezing Not suitable

To serve 6–8

1	Large onion	1
8 oz	Streaky bacon	225 g
1	Garlic clove	1
2 oz	Butter	50 g
8 oz	Long grain rice	225 g
3 pints	Light stock	1.7 litres
	Salt and pepper	
	Bouquet garni	
1 lb	Green cabbage	450 g
4 oz	Cheese	125 g

Peel and chop the onion; derind and finely dice the bacon. Peel and crush garlic. Melt the butter in a saucepan and add the onion, bacon and garlic. Fry gently for 5 minutes without browning.

Add the rice and cook, stirring, for 2 minutes till coated with butter. Add the stock, seasoning and bouquet garni. Bring to the boil and simmer for 15 minutes.

Meanwhile, coarsely shred the cabbage. Add to the pan, bring to the boil again and simmer for 5 minutes.

Remove pan from the heat and discard the bouquet garni. Grate cheese, stir into soup and adjust seasoning. Pour into a tureen and serve immediately with rye bread.

Chicken, lemon and egg drop soup

Overall timing 2 hours 10 minutes

Freezing Suitable: add eggs after reheating

To serve 6

1 lb	Knuckle of veal	450 g
3½ pints	Water	2 litres
3 lb	Boiling chicken with giblets	1.4 kg
1	Lemon	1
2	Onions	2
2	Cloves	2
	Salt and pepper	
2	Eggs	2

Place knuckle in saucepan with the water. Bring to the boil, then cover and simmer for 1 hour.

Meanwhile, chop the chicken into joints and remove skin if liked. Wash giblets. Grate the rind of the lemon and squeeze out the juice. Reserve both. Peel onions and spike each with a clove. Add chicken, giblets, lemon rind, spiked onions and seasoning to pan. Cover and cook gently for 1 hour till chicken is tender.

Strain the stock into a clean pan. Cut meats into small pieces, discarding bones, skin, giblets and onions. Skim stock, add meats and bring to the boil. Stir in lemon juice, then taste and adjust seasoning.

Beat the eggs in a small bowl. Remove saucepan from heat and pour soup into tureen. Drizzle egg in a thin stream into soup, stirring continuously. Serve.

Turkey vegetable soup

Overall timing 1¼ hours

Freezing Not suitable

To serve 6

1	Large carrot	1
1	Large onion	1
1	Stalk of celery	1
2	Turkey wings	2
2½ pints	Water	1.5 litres
	Salt and pepper	
8 oz	Waxy potatoes	225 g
2	Leeks	2
4	Thick slices of bread	4
3 oz	Butter	75 g

Peel and chop carrot and onion. Trim and chop the celery. Wipe the turkey wings and put into a saucepan with the prepared vegetables, water and seasoning. Bring to the boil, skim off any scum, cover and simmer for 45 minutes.

Peel potatoes and cut into ½ inch (12.5 mm) cubes. Trim and slice leeks.

Lift turkey wings out of pan with a draining spoon and leave to cool slightly. Add potatoes and leeks to the soup and simmer for 5 minutes till vegetables are tender.

Remove the skin and bones from the turkey wings and cut the flesh into strips. Add to the soup and reheat gently.

Meanwhile, remove the crusts from bread and cut into cubes. Melt butter in a frying pan, add the bread and fry till golden all over. Drain croûtons on kitchen paper.

Taste soup and adjust seasoning. Pour into a warmed tureen and sprinkle with croûtons. Serve immediately.

Tregaron broth

Overall timing 1 hour

Freezing Not suitable

To serve 6

1 lb	Streaky bacon	450 g
1 lb	Shin beef	450 g
1 oz	Butter	25 g
1	Large leek	1
1 lb	Potatoes	450 g
8 oz	Carrots	225 g
8 oz	Parsnips	225 g
1	Small swede	1
3 pints	Water	1.7 litres
1	Small white cabbage	1
2 oz	Fine or medium oatmeal	50 g
	Salt and pepper	

Derind the bacon and cut into 1 inch (2.5 cm) pieces. Trim the beef and cut into chunks. Melt the butter in a large saucepan and fry the bacon and beef for 5 minutes.

Meanwhile, trim and slice the leek. Peel the potatoes, carrots, parsnips and swede. Cut into chunks. Add vegetables to pan and fry for 5 minutes. Add the water and bring to the boil.

Shred the cabbage and add to the pan with the oatmeal and seasoning. Cover and simmer for 45 minutes. Adjust the seasoning to taste before serving.

Fish with orange

Overall timing 35 minutes

Freezing Not suitable

To serve 4

8	White fish fillets	8
	Salt and pepper	
2 tbsp	Plain flour	2x15 ml
4 oz	Butter	125 g
2	Oranges	2
1 tbsp	Chopped parsley	15 ml
	Sprigs of parsley	

Skin the fish fillets. Season the flour and use to coat the fish. Melt half the butter in frying pan, add half the fish fillets and fry for about 3 minutes each side.

Meanwhile, remove the rind and pith from one orange and divide the flesh into segments. Squeeze juice from remaining orange and reserve.

Remove the fish from the pan and keep hot while you cook the rest. Remove from the pan and keep hot.

Add remaining butter to the pan and heat gently until just beginning to brown. Add the orange juice and segments and the chopped parsley and mix well.

Return the fish to the pan and simmer for 2–3 minutes till tender. Arrange on a warmed serving dish and spoon the orange segments and pan juices over. Garnish with sprigs of parsley.

Fried plaice

Overall timing 30 minutes

Freezing Not suitable

To serve 6

3 oz	Unsalted butter	75 g
2 tbsp	Chopped parsley	2x15 ml
1 tbsp	Lemon juice	15 ml
	Salt and pepper	
3 tbsp	Plain flour	3x15 ml
3	Whole plaice, halved and boned	3
2	Eggs	2
4 oz	Golden breadcrumbs	125 g
	Oil for frying	
	Lemon slices	
	Sprigs of parsley	

Mash the butter with the chopped parsley and lemon juice. Shape into a roll and chill.

Season the flour and lightly coat the plaice. Beat the eggs in a shallow dish. Spread the breadcrumbs on a plate. Dip the fish into the egg so that it covers both sides. Dip into the crumbs, pressing them on lightly till evenly coated.

Heat the oil in a large frying pan and add two or three of the coated fillets, skin side up. Fry gently for 3–5 minutes, then turn the fish carefully and cook for a further 3–5 minutes till the fish is tender and the coating crisp. Lift out of the pan with a fish slice and drain on kitchen paper. Arrange on a warmed serving dish and keep hot while the rest of the fish is cooked.

Garnish with slices of parsley butter, lemon slices and sprigs of parsley. Serve with chips or sauté potatoes.

Baked cod with rosemary

Overall timing 45 minutes

Freezing Not suitable

To serve 4-6

2½ lb	End piece of cod	1.1 kg
4 tbsp	Oil	4x15 ml
8	Anchovy fillets	8
	Fresh rosemary	
4	Basil leaves (optional)	4
2 tbsp	Dried breadcrumbs	2x15 ml
	Salt and pepper	

Ask your fishmonger to remove bones from cod, leaving two halves attached at one side. Scale fish, using a descaler or the blunt side of a knife.

Preheat the oven to 350°F (180°C) Gas 4.

Heat half the oil in a flameproof casserole, add the chopped anchovies and heat through. Mash anchovies well, then transfer to a bowl. Put a little of the mashed anchovy mixture inside the fish, together with a few sprigs of fresh rosemary and the basil leaves, if using.

Place fish in the casserole and pour the remaining anchovy mixture and oil over. Add a little more rosemary and sprinkle with breadcrumbs, salt and pepper. Bake for about 30 minutes till the fish is cooked and the top is golden. Serve with boiled potatoes and a green vegetable or salad.

Cod with onions and leeks

Overall timing 35 minutes

Freezing Not suitable

To serve 4–6

1¾ lb	Cod fillets	750 g
3 tbsp	Lemon juice	3x15 ml
	Salt	
2	Large onions	2
2	Leeks	2
3 tbsp	Oil	3x15 ml
¼ pint	Dry cider	150 ml
2 tbsp	Chopped parsley	2x15 ml

Place cod fillets in a bowl with lemon juice and salt.

Peel and chop onions. Trim and chop leeks. Heat oil in a frying pan and cook onions and leeks gently till softened.

Add cod fillets, with any juices, and cider to pan and cook for 15 minutes till fish is cooked through. Sprinkle with parsley before serving with mashed potatoes.

Baked coley

Overall timing 1 hour

Freezing Not suitable

To serve 4

3 lb	Piece of coley	1.4 kg
1	Strip of bacon fat	1
2 oz	Butter	50 g
	Salt and pepper	
4	Smoked bacon rashers	4
1	Large can of flageolet beans	1
$\frac{1}{4}$ teasp	Dried sage	1.25 ml
$\frac{1}{4}$ pint	Chicken stock	150 ml

Preheat the oven to 425°F (220°C) Gas 7.

Roll up the coley and tie as you would a piece of beef, with the bacon fat wrapped round. Reserve a knob of butter and use most of the rest to grease a roasting tin. Place coley in it. Dot with more butter, season, then bake for 30 minutes.

Derind and chop bacon. Melt reserved knob of butter in saucepan and fry bacon till crisp. Drain can of beans and add to pan with sage and stock. Cook over a low heat for 10 minutes.

Put coley on a warmed serving plate. Arrange beans and bacon round coley and serve with parsleyed new potatoes.

Coley with spicy sauce

Overall timing 1 hour

Freezing Not suitable

To serve 4

4	Onions	4
4–6	Garlic cloves	4–6
1 lb	Tomatoes	450 g
1	Lemon	1
$\frac{1}{4}$ pint	Oil	150 ml
$\frac{1}{4}$ teasp	Cayenne	1.25 ml
4	Coley steaks	4
	Salt	
	Chopped parsley	

Peel and slice onions. Peel and crush garlic. Blanch, peel and chop tomatoes. Cut four thin slices from lemon and squeeze juice from remainder.

Heat oil in a saucepan. Add onions, garlic and tomatoes and cook gently for about 25 minutes.

Add cayenne and mix in well. Place coley steaks on top of mixture in pan. Sprinkle with salt and lemon juice, cover with lid and cook for a further 15 minutes, turning the fish steaks once.

Arrange coley steaks on a bed of rice on warmed serving dish. Spoon tomato mixture on top and garnish with lemon slices and chopped parsley.

Hake au gratin

Overall timing 30 minutes

Freezing Not suitable

To serve 4

1	Small onion	1
2 tbsp	Chopped parsley	2x15 ml
1¾ lb	Hake steaks	750 g
	Salt and pepper	
	Grated nutmeg	
2 tbsp	Lemon juice	2x15 ml
1 oz	Butter	25 g
4 oz	Cheese	125 g
2 oz	Fresh breadcrumbs	50 g

Preheat oven to 375°F (190°C) Gas 5.

Peel and chop onion and place in a shallow ovenproof dish with half the parsley and the fish steaks. Season with salt and pepper and a pinch of nutmeg. Sprinkle the lemon juice over the fish and dot with butter. Grate the cheese and mix with the breadcrumbs and remaining parsley. Sprinkle over the fish. Bake for about 20 minutes.

Remove from oven and baste with liquid in dish. Bake for another 10 minutes until topping is golden. Serve immediately with jacket-baked potatoes.

Fried mackerel with apple cream sauce

Overall timing 45 minutes

Freezing Not suitable

To serve 4

2x1½ lb	Mackerel	2x700 g
6 tbsp	Plain flour	6x15 ml
1 teasp	Mild curry powder	5 ml
	Salt and pepper	
1	Large cooking apple	1
4 oz	Butter	125 g
3 tbsp	Oil	3x15 ml
1 teasp	Caster sugar	5 ml
¼ pint	Carton of double cream	150 ml
2	Egg yolks	2

Cut mackerel into 2 inch (5 cm) thick steaks, discarding the heads and tails. Mix the flour, curry powder and seasoning together in a polythene bag. Add the fish steaks and toss lightly till evenly coated.

Peel, core and chop the cooking apple. Melt 2 oz (50 g) of the butter in a saucepan, add the apple and stir till coated. Cover and sweat over a low heat for 5–10 minutes till pulpy.

Melt the remaining butter with the oil in a frying pan. Add the mackerel steaks and fry over a moderate heat for about 15 minutes, turning frequently, till the flesh is tender and the skin is crisp and golden.

Meanwhile, rub the apple through a sieve into a clean pan. Add the sugar and stir till dissolved. Beat the cream into the egg yolks, then add to the apple purée. Stir over a low heat for 3 minutes without boiling till the mixture is smooth and thick. Add salt and pepper to taste.

Pour the sauce into a warmed sauceboat and serve immediately with the fried fish, new potatoes and buttered carrots or minted peas.

Kippers with apple

Overall timing 15 minutes plus marination

Freezing Not suitable

To serve 4

6	Kipper fillets	6
½ pint	Milk	300 ml
1	Apple	1
2	Onions	2
2	Hard-boiled eggs	2
5 tbsp	Double cream	5x15 ml
1 tbsp	French mustard	15 ml
	Salt and pepper	

Place kipper fillets in a glass or pottery bowl. Bring milk just to the boil, pour over kippers and leave for 3 hours.

Peel, core and chop the apple. Peel the onions; chop one and slice the other. Shell and slice the eggs.

Drain kippers, pat dry with kitchen paper, then cut into pieces and place in a serving dish. Mix together cream, mustard, chopped onion and seasoning. Pour mixture over kippers and mix well.

Garnish with onion rings and slices of hard-boiled egg and serve with wholemeal bread.

Grilled fish steaks

Overall timing 20 minutes plus marination

Freezing Not suitable

To serve 6

6x6 oz	White fish steaks	6x175 g
3 tbsp	Oil	3x15 ml
3 tbsp	Lemon juice	3x15 ml
	Salt and pepper	
	Sprig of rosemary	
Sauce		
¼ pint	Oil	150 ml
4 tbsp	Hot water	4x15 ml
3 tbsp	Lemon juice	3x15 ml
2	Garlic cloves	2
3 tbsp	Chopped parsley	3x15 ml
	Salt and pepper	

Place fish steaks on a large plate and sprinkle with oil, lemon juice and seasoning. Marinate for 2 hours.

Preheat the grill.

Lift fish steaks out of marinade and place on grill rack. Dip rosemary into marinade and brush over fish. Grill for 15 minutes till tender, turning once.

Meanwhile, make sauce. Put oil into a bowl and beat in hot water. Add lemon juice, peeled and crushed garlic, parsley and seasoning. Stand bowl over a pan of simmering water and whisk for 3 minutes.

Arrange fish on a serving dish and spoon sauce over.

Rollmops

Overall timing 30 minutes plus 48 hours soaking and 4 days standing

Freezing Not suitable

To serve 6

4	Filleted fresh herrings	4
2 pints	Water	1.1 litre
8 oz	Salt	225 g
2 tbsp	Capers	2x15 ml
2	Onions	2
1	Large gherkin	1
4 teasp	Made mustard	4x5 ml
Marinade		
½ pint	Cider vinegar	300 ml
½ pint	Water	300 ml
1	Bay leaf	1
10	Black peppercorns	10
2	Cloves	2
5	Juniper berries	5
1 teasp	Mustard seed	5 ml

Soak herrings in half water and salt for 24 hours. Drain and repeat.

Put all marinade ingredients into a pan. Bring to the boil and boil for 5 minutes. Cool.

Chop capers. Peel onions and cut into rings. Quarter gherkin lengthways. Drain and rinse herrings. Lay skin down and spread with mustard. Sprinkle with capers and onion rings. Add gherkin and roll up. Pour over marinade. Leave 4 days before eating.

Marinated sprats

Overall timing 45 minutes plus overnight marination

Freezing Not suitable

To serve 6

2 lb	Sprats	900 g
	Salt and pepper	
3 oz	Plain flour	75 g
	Oil for frying	
1	Large onion	1
8	Sage leaves	8
6 tbsp	Vinegar	6x15 ml
4 tbsp	Water	4x15 ml

Clean the fish through the gills. Rinse and drain thoroughly. Season the flour and use to coat the fish. Heat 1 inch (2.5 cm) oil in a deep frying pan and fry the floured sprats, a few at a time, for about 4 minutes till crisp and golden. Drain on kitchen paper, then put into a shallow serving dish.

Peel and slice the onion. Heat 2 tbsp (2x15 ml) oil in frying pan, add the onion and fry gently till transparent. Add the sage leaves, vinegar and water and bring to the boil. Boil for 3 minutes, then remove from the heat and season.

Pour the hot marinade over the sprats. Cover and leave to marinate in a cool place overnight. Serve cold with crusty bread and butter.

Mackerel in mushroom sauce

Overall timing 40 minutes

Freezing Not suitable

To serve 4

8 oz	Button mushrooms	225 g
2	Onions	2
1	Garlic clove	1
12 oz	Tomatoes	350 g
5 tbsp	Oil	5x15 ml
	Salt and pepper	
2 tbsp	White wine vinegar	2x15 ml
2 lb	Mackerel fillets	900 g
2 tbsp	Plain flour	2x15 ml

Slice mushrooms. Peel and finely chop onions. Peel and crush garlic. Wash tomatoes and cut into $\frac{1}{2}$ inch (12.5 mm) thick slices.

Heat 2 tbsp (2x15 ml) of the oil in a saucepan. Add onions, mushrooms and garlic and fry for 10 minutes, stirring frequently. Season. Stir in the vinegar and boil rapidly till it evaporates.

Coat fillets with seasoned flour. Heat the remaining oil in a large frying pan, add the fillets and fry for 5 minutes on each side. Drain, arrange on a warmed serving dish and keep hot.

Add tomato slices to frying pan and fry for 2 minutes. Spoon mushroom mixture over fillets. Season tomatoes and arrange on top. Serve immediately with minted peas.

Fish lasagne

Overall timing 1¼ hours

Freezing Suitable: reheat from frozen in 350°F (180°C) Gas 4 oven for 1 hour

To serve 4

1½ lb	Prepared mackerel	700 g
1	Onion	1
3 fl oz	Oil	90 ml
2	Garlic cloves	2
2 tbsp	Tomato purée	2x15 ml
	Salt and pepper	
1 lb	Fresh peas	450 g
4 oz	Mushrooms	125 g
8 oz	Lasagne	225 g
2 tbsp	Grated Parmesan cheese	2x15 ml
2 tbsp	Chopped parsley	2x15 ml

Cut fish into large pieces. Peel and chop onion. Heat 3 tbsp (3x15 ml) of oil in saucepan, add onion and fry until golden. Add fish and cook for 5 minutes, turning once.

Peel and crush garlic. Stir tomato purée into ¼ pint (150 ml) of water and add to pan with half garlic and seasoning. Cover and cook gently for 10 minutes.

Shell peas. Slice mushrooms. Heat 2 tbsp (2x15 ml) of oil in another saucepan, add peas, mushrooms and other half of garlic and cook for 5 minutes. Add 3 fl oz (90 ml) of water and seasoning, cover and cook for 10 minutes.

Meanwhile, cook lasagne in boiling salted water for 10–15 minutes or till tender. Drain thoroughly.

Preheat oven to 350°F (180°C) Gas 4.

Remove fish from pan and cut into pieces, discarding bones. Return to pan with mushroom mixture. Gradually stir in Parmesan and parsley.

Line greased ovenproof dish with one-third of lasagne, cover with one-third of fish mixture and sprinkle with a little oil. Repeat layers, finishing with fish mixture. Sprinkle with oil and bake for 20 minutes.

Beef and onion stew

Overall timing 2 hours

Freezing Suitable: simmer for only 30 minutes before freezing

To serve 6

2 lb	Stewing beef	900 g
	Salt and pepper	
3 tbsp	Plain flour	3x15 ml
2 oz	Lard	50 g
1 lb	Onions	450 g
½ pint	Lager	300 ml
2 tbsp	Tomato purée	2x15 ml
1 tbsp	Chopped parsley	15 ml
1 teasp	Dried thyme	5 ml

Cut the meat into cubes. Season the flour and toss the meat in it till lightly coated. Melt the lard in a flameproof casserole and fry the meat for 10 minutes, turning occasionally till browned on all sides. Remove meat from pan and reserve.

Peel and thinly slice the onions and fry in casserole till golden. Sprinkle in the remaining flour and cook, stirring, till pale golden. Gradually add the lager and bring to the boil, stirring constantly. Add the tomato purée, seasoning, parsley and thyme. Return meat to casserole. Stir, cover tightly and simmer for about 1½ hours till the meat is tender.

Taste and adjust the seasoning and serve immediately with creamed potatoes and a green vegetable.

Flemish hotpot

Overall timing 3¾ hours

Freezing Not suitable

To serve 6

2	Pig's trotters	2
1 lb	Piece of belly of pork	450 g
1 lb	Beef flank	450 g
5 pints	Water	2.8 litres
1 tbsp	Salt	15 ml
2	Bay leaves	2
12	Peppercorns	12
3	Onions	3
4	Cloves	4
1½ lb	Potatoes	700 g
1 lb	Carrots	450 g
1 lb	Cabbage *or*	450 g
12 oz	Spinach	350 g

Split trotters lengthways, then halve each half. Cut belly of pork into 3x2 inch (7.5x5 cm) strips. Roll up beef and tie with string. Put water into a large pan and add meats with salt, bay leaves and peppercorns. Peel onions and spike one with cloves. Add it to pan and bring to the boil. Skim and simmer for 2 hours.

Remove meats from pan. Strain stock and return to pan with meats.

Peel and chop potatoes. Scrape and thickly slice carrots. Chop cabbage or spinach. Quarter remaining onions. Bring stock to the boil and add vegetables. Simmer for 20–25 minutes till vegetables are tender.

Lift meats out of stock. Remove string from beef and carve into thick slices. Strain off 1 pint (560 ml) of the stock and reserve.

Taste the soup and adjust the seasoning. Pour into a warmed tureen and serve immediately. Serve the meats after the soup with reserved stock thickened and made into gravy.

Steamed steak and kidney pudding

Overall timing 5¾ hours

Freezing Suitable: steam from frozen for 2½–3 hours

To serve 6

1½ lb	Chuck or blade steak	700 g
8 oz	Ox kidney	225 g
1	Large onion	1
	Salt and pepper	
3 tbsp	Plain flour	3x15 ml
12 oz	Self-raising flour	350 g
6 oz	Shredded suet	175 g
½ pint	Cold beef stock	300 ml

Cut the meat into 1½ inch (4 cm) cubes. Trim the kidney, removing any core, and cut into 1 inch (2.5 cm) cubes. Peel and thinly slice the onion. Season plain flour and use to coat the steak, kidney and onion.

Sift the self-raising flour and 1½ teasp (7.5 ml) salt into a bowl and stir in the suet and enough cold water to mix to a soft but not sticky dough. Knead lightly till smooth.

Roll out on a floured surface to a round, big enough to line a 3 pint (1.7 litre) pudding basin (about 14 inches/35 cm in diameter). Cut out one-quarter of the dough round and reserve. Lift the large piece and place it in the basin, curving it so it fits neatly, and sealing the edges together. Place the meat mixture in the basin and add the cold stock to come half-way up the meat.

Roll out the reserved dough to a round slightly larger than the top of the basin. Brush the top edge of the dough lining with water and cover with the dough lid. Seal the edges well.

Cover with greased, pleated greaseproof paper and pleated foil, or a pudding cloth and secure with string. Steam for 5 hours, topping up with boiling water as required.

Mustardy beef rissoles

Overall timing 25 minutes

Freezing Suitable: fry from frozen for 15 minutes

To serve 4

2	Large onions	2
1	Carrot	1
1 lb	Minced beef	450 g
1 tbsp	Chopped parsley	15 ml
1	Egg	1
2 teasp	Mustard seeds	2x5 ml
	Salt and pepper	
3 tbsp	Plain flour	3x15 ml
4 tbsp	Oil	4x15 ml
	Sprigs of parsley	

Peel and finely chop the onions. Peel and finely grate the carrot. Put into a bowl with the minced beef, parsley and egg.

Roughly grind the mustard seed in a mortar or pepper mill and add to the beef with plenty of salt and pepper. Mix with a fork till the ingredients are well blended. Shape into 12 balls and coat with seasoned flour.

Heat the oil in a frying pan and fry the meatballs for about 10 minutes till crisp and golden on all sides. Drain on kitchen paper and arrange on a warmed serving plate. Garnish with sprigs of parsley.

Beef and bean casserole

Overall timing 3 hours plus soaking

Freezing Suitable: reheat from frozen in 325°F (170°C) Gas 3 oven

To serve 4–6

8 oz	Dried haricot beans	225 g
2	Onions	2
2 tbsp	Oil	2x15 ml
1 lb	Stewing beef	450 g
¼ teasp	Chilli powder	1.25 ml
1 teasp	Curry powder	5 ml
2 tbsp	Plain flour	2x15 ml
½ pint	Beef stock	300 ml
14 oz	Can of tomatoes	397 g
2 tbsp	Tomato purée	2x15 ml
2 teasp	Sugar	2x5 ml
	Salt and pepper	
1	Large cooking apple	1
2 oz	Sultanas	50 g

Put beans in a large saucepan and cover with cold water. Bring to the boil. Boil for 2 minutes, then remove from the heat, cover and leave to soak for 2 hours.

Preheat the oven to 325°F (170°C) Gas 3.

Peel and chop onions. Heat oil in a flame-proof casserole and fry onions for 3 minutes. Cut beef into chunks. Add to pan and fry quickly till brown. Stir in the chilli and curry powder and flour. Fry for 2 minutes.

Gradually add stock and bring to the boil, stirring. Add the tomatoes with their juice and tomato purée. Drain beans and add to casserole with the sugar and seasoning. Cover and cook in the oven for 2 hours.

Peel, core and chop apple. Stir into casserole with sultanas and cook for a further 30 minutes. Taste and adjust seasoning. Serve with crusty bread.

Corned beef hash

Overall timing 1 hour

Freezing Not suitable

To serve 4

2	Medium-size onions	2
6 tbsp	Oil *or*	6x15 ml
2 oz	Dripping	50 g
1	Stalk of celery	1
1	Large carrot	1
1 lb	Corned beef	450 g
	Salt and pepper	
½ teasp	Powdered mustard	2.5 ml
1 lb	Potatoes	450 g
1 pint	Beef stock	560 ml

Peel and thinly slice onions. Heat oil or dripping in saucepan. Add the onions and cook gently till transparent.

Finely chop celery. Peel and grate or dice carrot. Cut corned beef into 1 inch (2.5 cm) cubes. Add all of these to onions and cook for a few minutes, then season with salt, pepper and mustard (add more if a stronger taste is preferred). Cook gently for 5 minutes.

Meanwhile, peel potatoes and cut into chunks. Add to pan with boiling stock and cook for 20 minutes. Serve in warm bowls topped with fried or poached eggs, and with lots of fresh bread to mop up the juices.

Chillied pork chops

Overall timing 1½ hours

Freezing Suitable

To serve 4

12 oz	Lentils	350 g
2	Onions	2
1	Clove	1
1	Carrot	1
	Bouquet garni	
	Salt and pepper	
2	Garlic cloves	2
1	Fresh red chilli	1
1 oz	Butter	25 g
1 tbsp	Oil	15 ml
4	Pork chops	4
8 oz	Can of tomatoes	227 g
1 tbsp	Tomato purée	15 ml

Put lentils into a large saucepan and cover with 2½ pints (1.5 litres) water. Bring to the boil and boil for 5 minutes.

Peel onions. Spike one with the clove. Scrape and halve carrot. Drain lentils. Cover with 2½ pints (1.5 litres) fresh water, bring to the boil and add spiked onion, carrot and bouquet garni. Simmer for 30 minutes. Add salt and cook for a further 30 minutes.

Drain lentils. Discard spiked onion and bouquet garni.

Chop the other onion; peel and chop garlic. Deseed and thinly slice chilli.

Heat butter and oil in pan and lightly brown chops on both sides. Remove. Fry onion, garlic and chilli till golden. Remove chilli.

Add lentils, then chops and cook for a few minutes, stirring occasionally. Season. Sieve tomatoes with their juice and tomato purée. Pour over chops and lentils. Cover and simmer for 10–15 minutes. Remove lid and cook till sauce evaporates slightly. Garnish with chilli.

Roast pork with oranges

Overall timing 2¼ hours

Freezing Not suitable

To serve 6–8

3 lb	Rolled spare rib of pork	1.4 kg
1 oz	Butter	25 g
	Salt and pepper	
5	Oranges	5
2 tbsp	Lemon juice	2x15 ml
¼ pint	Hot water	150 ml
6	Sugar lumps	6
1 tbsp	Wine vinegar	15 ml
2 teasp	Arrowroot	2x5 ml

Preheat the oven to 450°F (230°C) Gas 8.

Place pork in a roasting tin. Spread butter over lean parts and rub salt and pepper into skin. Roast for 20 minutes.

Meanwhile, squeeze juice from two oranges.

Peel remaining oranges. Cut two into slices and one into segments.

Remove pork from tin and keep warm. Pour off any fat from tin and add orange and lemon juices and water. Stir well, scraping any sediment from bottom of tin. Reduce oven temperature to 400°F (200°C) Gas 6.

Replace meat in tin and roast for a further 1½ hours, basting occasionally.

Meanwhile, put sugar lumps into a saucepan with 1 tbsp (15 ml) water. Stir till dissolved, then boil rapidly, without stirring, till golden. Remove from heat and stir in vinegar. Return to heat and stir till caramel dissolves.

Place pork on a warmed serving dish. Stir cooking liquor from tin into caramel. Blend arrowroot with 2 tbsp (2x15 ml) water and add to caramel. Bring to the boil, stirring. Add the sliced and segmented oranges. Heat through for 1–2 minutes.

Cut pork into thick slices and arrange the pieces of orange around. Serve the sauce separately in a warmed sauceboat.

Sausage surprise

Overall timing 35 minutes

Freezing Not suitable

To serve 4–6

2 lb	Potatoes	900 g
	Salt and pepper	
1 lb	Chipolatas	450 g
½ pint	Milk	300 ml
2 oz	Butter	50 g
6 oz	Cheese	175 g
½ teasp	Grated nutmeg	2.5 ml

Preheat the grill. Peel the potatoes and cut into quarters. Cook in boiling salted water for about 10 minutes till tender.

Meanwhile, grill the chipolatas for about 15 minutes, turning occasionally till well browned.

Drain the potatoes in a colander. Add the milk to the pan and bring just to the boil. Return the potatoes to the pan with the butter and mash till smooth.

Grate cheese and beat 4 oz (125 g) into potatoes with nutmeg and seasoning. Spread the mixture in a flameproof dish and push the chipolatas diagonally into the potato so that the tops are just showing.

Sprinkle the remaining cheese over and grill for about 5 minutes till golden.

Bacon with lentils

Overall timing 2½ hours plus 3 hours soaking

Freezing Not suitable

To serve 6

2¼ lb	Middle cut bacon hock	1 kg
1	Carrot	1
2	Onions	2
1	Garlic clove	1
	Bouquet garni	
8	Peppercorns	8
1 lb	Continental lentils	450 g
	Salt and pepper	

Put bacon joint in a large saucepan and cover with cold water. Soak for 3 hours, changing the water several times.

Drain the bacon joint and cover with fresh water. Peel and slice the carrot; peel and quarter the onions; peel and halve the garlic. Add to the bacon with the bouquet garni and peppercorns. Bring to the boil, cover and simmer for 45 minutes.

Remove bouquet garni. Wash and pick over lentils. Add to bacon, cover and cook for a further hour till lentils are tender. Adjust seasoning, then arrange on warmed dish and serve with mustard.

Lamb stew

Overall timing 2 hours

Freezing Suitable: add potatoes after reheating

To serve 4

2 oz	Butter	50 g
1 tbsp	Oil	15 ml
2½ lb	Middle neck lamb chops	1.1 kg
2 tbsp	Plain flour	2x15 ml
½ pint	Stock or water	300 ml
8 oz	Turnips	225 g
2	Onions	2
8 oz	Carrots	225 g
1	Stalk of celery	1
	Bouquet garni	
	Salt and pepper	
1 lb	Potatoes	450 g

Heat the butter and oil in a flameproof casserole, add the chops and brown well on all sides. Sprinkle flour over and cook, stirring, for 3 minutes. Gradually stir in stock or water.

Peel and chop turnips and onions. Peel carrots and cut into pieces lengthways. Add to casserole with celery stalk, bouquet garni and seasoning. Cover and cook for 1½ hours over low heat.

Peel potatoes and cut into large chunks. Add to casserole and cook, covered, for a further 20 minutes. Discard bouquet garni before serving.

Lamb with cauliflower

Overall timing 1½ hours

Freezing Not suitable

To serve 6

1	Small cauliflower	1
½ pint	Water	300 ml
	Salt and pepper	
8 oz	Tomatoes	225 g
1	Large onion	1
2	Garlic cloves	2
2 tbsp	Oil	2x15 ml
2 lb	Breast of lamb riblets	900 g
¼ pint	Tomato juice	150 ml

Trim cauliflower and divide into florets. Bring water and ½ teasp (2.5 ml) salt to the boil in a saucepan, add cauliflower and cook for 5 minutes. Drain, reserving cooking liquor.

Blanch, peel and chop tomatoes. Peel and chop onion. Peel and crush garlic. Heat the oil and garlic in a saucepan, add onion and cook till transparent. Season meat, add to pan and brown quickly on all sides over a high heat, turning frequently to prevent the riblets burning.

Add tomatoes to pan with reserved cooking liquor and tomato juice. Bring to the boil. Add pepper and cook, covered, for 1 hour.

Add cauliflower and cook for a further 15 minutes. Adjust seasoning, then serve with boiled potatoes.

Shepherds' pie

Overall timing 1 hour

Freezing Not suitable

To serve 4

2 lb	Potatoes	900 g
	Salt and pepper	
1	Large onion	1
3 tbsp	Oil	3 x 15 ml
1	Garlic clove	1
1 lb	Minced cooked lamb	450 g
2 oz	Butter	50 g
$\frac{1}{4}$ pint	Milk	150 ml
3 oz	Cheese	75 g

Peel and halve potatoes. Cook in boiling salted water for 25–30 minutes.

Peel and finely chop onion. Heat oil in a frying pan, add onion and cook for about 10 minutes. Peel and crush garlic. Add garlic and meat to pan and cook for about 5 minutes, stirring.

Preheat the oven to 425°F (220°C) Gas 7.

Drain potatoes and mash with half the butter and the milk. Season to taste. Cover bottom of ovenproof dish with half of the mashed potato, cover with the meat, then spread or pipe the remaining potato on top.

Grate cheese. Sprinkle over potato, dot with remaining butter and bake for about 15 minutes till the top is browned. Serve with green salad.

Welsh chicken and mace pie

Overall timing 1 hour

Freezing Not suitable

To serve 6

1½ lb	Cooked chicken	700 g
4 oz	Cooked tongue	125 g
1	Onion	1
4	Leeks	4
3	Stalks of celery	3
2 oz	Butter	50 g
1 teasp	Ground mace	5 ml
1 tbsp	Chopped parsley	15 ml
½ pint	Chicken stock	300 ml
	Salt and pepper	
12 oz	Shortcrust pastry	350 g
1	Egg	1

Preheat oven to 400°F (200°C) Gas 6.

Chop chicken into medium-size pieces. Cut the tongue into strips. Peel and thinly slice onion. Trim leeks, then cut into thin slices. Trim and finely chop the celery. Melt butter.

Put chicken, tongue and prepared vegetables in a bowl with mace, parsley and butter and mix well. Place in a large pie dish and add stock and seasoning.

Roll out dough and place on dish. Press edge to dish to seal. Lightly beat the egg and brush over the dough. Bake for 40 minutes, or until the pastry is golden. Serve immediately with mashed potatoes.

Poule-au-pot

Overall timing 4 hours

Freezing Not suitable

To serve 6

2 oz	Streaky bacon	50 g
4 oz	Pork sausagemeat	125 g
2 oz	Fresh breadcrumbs	50 g
2 tbsp	Chopped parsley	2x15 ml
	Salt and pepper	
2	Eggs	2
3½ lb	Boiling chicken	1.6 kg
4	Medium-size onions	4
4	Small turnips	4
6	Large carrots	6
2	Leeks	2
4	Stalks of celery	4
2 oz	Dripping	50 g
	Bouquet garni	
12 oz	Long grain rice	350 g

Derind bacon, reserving rinds, and chop finely. Mix sausagemeat, bacon, breadcrumbs, parsley and seasoning and bind with eggs. Spoon into chicken and truss.

Peel onions, turnips and carrots. Trim leeks and celery. Heat dripping in a large pan and brown chicken all over. Add one of the onions, turnips, leeks and celery stalks and two carrots and fry for 3 minutes. Pour off excess fat.

Add bouquet garni, bacon rinds, giblets and cold water to cover the chicken and bring to the boil. Skim off any scum. Cover and simmer for about 2¼ hours.

Discard vegetables, bacon rinds and bouquet garni. Add remaining vegetables and seasoning. Cover and simmer for a further 45 minutes. Remove from heat. Strain 2¼ pints (1.3 litres) of stock into another saucepan. Keep chicken hot.

Add rice to stock with salt and cover tightly. Bring to boil and simmer for 15–20 minutes till rice is tender.

Fluff rice and arrange on a serving dish. Place chicken on rice and discard trussing strings. Arrange vegetables around chicken and serve.

Chicken with lentils

Overall timing 1¼ hours

Freezing Not suitable

To serve 6

12 oz	Continental lentils	350 g
1	Onion	1
1	Carrot	1
	Bouquet garni	
	Salt and pepper	
1 lb	Boned chicken	450 g
1 tbsp	Oil	15 ml
3 oz	Butter	75 g
1 tbsp	Chopped parsley	15 ml

Wash and pick over lentils. Place in a saucepan and add enough cold water just to cover. Peel and finely chop onion. Peel and halve carrot. Add to lentils with bouquet garni and seasoning. Bring to boil, cover and simmer for 35 minutes.

Meanwhile, cut chicken into neat pieces. Heat oil and half the butter in a frying pan, add chicken pieces and fry for 5 minutes, turning once. Add chicken to lentils, cover and simmer for a further 30 minutes.

Discard bouquet garni and carrot. Stir the remaining butter into lentils. Taste and adjust seasoning. Arrange chicken and lentils on a warmed serving dish and sprinkle with parsley. Serve immediately with a mixed salad.

Sweetbread kebabs

Overall timing 35 minutes plus marination

Freezing Not suitable

To serve 4

1 lb	Prepared lambs' sweetbreads	450 g
4	Thick streaky bacon rashers	4
6 tbsp	Oil	6x15 ml
1 tbsp	Lemon juice	15 ml
	Salt and pepper	
$\frac{1}{2}$	Lemon	$\frac{1}{2}$
	Sprigs of parsley	

Cut the sweetbreads in half. Derind the bacon and cut into 1 inch (2.5 cm) pieces. Thread the sweetbreads and bacon alternately on to four greased skewers.

Mix the oil, lemon juice and seasoning in a shallow dish. Add the kebabs, turning them to coat with the marinade. Leave in a cool place for 1 hour.

Preheat the grill. Place each kebab on a piece of foil, shaping the foil into a dish so it will hold the marinade, and pour the marinade over. Arrange the kebabs on the grill pan and grill for 15–20 minutes, turning frequently in the marinade, till the sweetbreads are tender.

Arrange the kebabs on a warmed serving dish and pour the marinade over. Garnish with the lemon and parsley and serve immediately with crusty bread.

Tripe and onions French style

Overall timing 1 hour 50 minutes

Freezing Not suitable

To serve 4

1	Large carrot	1
1½ lb	Onions	700 g
2	Stalks of celery	2
3 pints	Cold water	1.7 litres
	Bay leaf	
6	Peppercorns	6
1 tbsp	Lemon juice	15 ml
1½ lb	Dressed tripe	700 g
3 oz	Butter	75 g
	Salt and pepper	
2 tbsp	Chopped parsley	2 x 15 ml
2 tbsp	White wine vinegar	2 x 15 ml

Peel and chop carrot and one of the onions. Trim and chop celery. Put into a saucepan with water, bay leaf, peppercorns and lemon juice. Bring to the boil and simmer for 30 minutes. Strain and return to pan.

Cut tripe into pieces. Place in pan with stock and bring to the boil. Skim off any scum, cover and simmer for 1½ hours till tender.

Peel and slice remaining onions. Melt butter in a frying pan, add the onions and fry gently till golden.

Drain the tripe thoroughly, discarding the stock, and cut into thin strips. Add to the onions with plenty of seasoning and fry over a moderate heat for 10 minutes, stirring frequently. Add the parsley and vinegar and mix lightly. Season to taste and pour into a warmed serving dish. Serve immediately with crusty bread.

Macaroni with cheese

Overall timing 45 minutes

Freezing Not suitable

To serve 4

12 oz	Short-cut macaroni	350 g
	Salt and pepper	
3 oz	Butter	75 g
2 oz	Plain flour	50 g
¾ pint	Milk	400 ml
4 tbsp	Grated Parmesan cheese	4x15 ml
2 tbsp	Dried breadcrumbs	2x15 ml

Cook macaroni in boiling salted water till tender. Drain in colander and return to saucepan. Stir in 1 oz (25 g) of the butter and seasoning.

Preheat oven to 350°F (180°C) Gas 4.

Melt remaining butter in a saucepan, stir in flour and cook for 1 minute. Gradually add the milk and bring to the boil. Cook, stirring constantly, until sauce is thick and smooth. Season to taste.

Transfer macaroni to greased ovenproof dish, cover with sauce and sprinkle the Parmesan and breadcrumbs on top. Bake for 20 minutes till top is crisp and golden. Serve immediately.

Spaghetti with sardine dressing

Overall timing 20 minutes

Freezing Not suitable

To serve 4

12 oz	Spaghetti	350 g
	Salt and pepper	
11½ oz	Can of sardines	326 g
2	Garlic cloves	2
3 oz	Butter	75 g

Cook the spaghetti in boiling salted water till tender.

Drain the sardines and put into a mortar. Peel and crush garlic and add to sardines. Pound to a paste with a pestle. Add the butter and mix well. Season to taste.

Drain the spaghetti and return to the pan. Add the sardine paste and toss lightly over a low heat till the spaghetti is coated. Place in a warmed serving dish and serve immediately with wedges of lemon.

Spaghetti alla carbonara

Overall timing 20 minutes

Freezing Not suitable

To serve 4

12 oz	Spaghetti	350 g
	Salt and pepper	
2	Eggs	2
2 tbsp	Top of the milk	2 x 15 ml
4 oz	Streaky bacon rashers	125 g
1 tbsp	Oil	15 ml
2 oz	Grated Parmesan cheese	50 g

Cook the spaghetti in boiling salted water till tender.

Meanwhile, beat eggs, milk and pepper in a bowl. Derind and dice the bacon. Heat the oil in large frying pan, add the bacon and fry till crisp.

Drain the spaghetti and add to the bacon. Pour in the egg mixture, stirring, and toss over a gentle heat till the eggs just begin to set. Serve immediately, sprinkled with grated Parmesan.

Mushroom ravioli

Overall timing 45 minutes

Freezing Suitable: cook from frozen

To serve 4

12 oz	Strong flour	350 g
	Salt and pepper	
3	Eggs	3
1 lb	Mushrooms	450 g
1	Onion	1
2 oz	Butter	50 g

Sift flour and 1 teasp (5 ml) salt into a bowl. Add eggs and mix to a smooth, glossy dough.

Chop the mushrooms. Peel and finely chop onion. Melt half the butter in a frying pan and fry the onion for 5 minutes till transparent. Add mushrooms and seasoning and stir-fry over a high heat for about 5 minutes to evaporate any liquid. Reduce heat and cook gently for a further 5 minutes. Remove from heat and leave to cool.

Roll out the dough on a lightly floured surface and cut into 3 inch (7.5 cm) squares with a pastry wheel. Divide the mushroom mixture between the squares, then fold them over, pressing the edges together well to seal.

Put plenty of lightly salted water in a large saucepan and bring to the boil. Add the ravioli and cook for 10–15 minutes, then drain and place in a warmed serving dish. Melt the remaining butter, pour over the ravioli and toss well.

Tagliatelli with ham

Overall timing 25 minutes

Freezing Not suitable

To serve 4

12 oz	Tagliatelli	350 g
	Salt and pepper	
1	Large onion	1
2 oz	Butter	50 g
2 tbsp	Oil	2x15 ml
1	Garlic clove	1
4 oz	Lean cooked ham	125 g
2 teasp	Dried marjoram	2x5 ml
14 oz	Can of tomatoes	397 g
6 tbsp	Grated Parmesan cheese	6x15 ml

Cook the tagliatelli in boiling salted water till tender.

Meanwhile, peel and finely chop the onion. Heat the butter and oil in a large saucepan and fry the onion till transparent. Peel and crush the garlic and add to the pan. Chop the ham very finely and add to the pan with the marjoram and tomatoes with their juice. Season and cook for 10 minutes, stirring to break up the tomatoes.

Drain the tagliatelli and place in a warmed bowl. Add the sauce and Parmesan and toss well, adding seasoning to taste. Serve immediately with a watercress, cucumber and lettuce salad.

Spaghetti omelette

Overall timing 30 minutes

Freezing Not suitable

To serve 4–6

12 oz	Spaghetti	350 g
	Salt and pepper	
1 oz	Cheddar cheese	25 g
1	Garlic clove	1
1 oz	Grated Parmesan cheese	25 g
4	Eggs	4
1 tbsp	Chopped parsley	15 ml
6	Basil leaves	6
2 oz	Butter	50 g

Cook the spaghetti in boiling salted water till tender.

Meanwhile, grate the Cheddar cheese. Peel and crush the garlic. Mix together the garlic, cheeses, eggs, parsley, chopped basil and seasoning.

Drain the spaghetti and put into a large bowl. Pour the egg and cheese mixture over and mix well. Melt 1 oz (25 g) butter in frying pan. Add spaghetti mixture and press down well with the back of a spoon to form a cake. Fry over a low heat for about 5 minutes, pressing down to keep the cake flat.

Run a knife round the edge of the omelette to loosen it, then turn it out on to a board. Add remaining butter to the pan and, when melted, slide the omelette back into the pan. Fry for 3–5 minutes till firmly set. Place on a warmed serving dish and serve immediately, cut into wedges.

Quiche lorraine

Overall timing 1½ hours

Freezing Suitable: reheat in hot oven

To serve 4–6

8 oz	Plain flour	225 g
	Salt and pepper	
5 oz	Butter	150 g
2 tbsp	Water	2x15 ml
2	Throughcut bacon rashers	2
3 oz	Cheddar cheese	75 g
2	Eggs	2
½ pint	Milk or single cream	300 ml

Sift the flour, salt and pepper into a bowl. Rub in 4 oz (125 g) of the butter till mixture resembles breadcrumbs. Gradually add the water and knead to a dough. Roll out and use to line a greased 8 inch (20 cm) pie plate or flan dish. Leave to stand for 30 minutes.

Preheat the oven to 400°F (200°C) Gas 6.

Derind and dice the bacon. Fry lightly in the remaining butter. Grate or thinly slice the cheese. Sprinkle bacon and cheese over the bottom of the flan case. Beat together the eggs, milk or cream and seasoning in a bowl. Pour mixture into flan. Do not overfill.

Bake for 15 minutes, then reduce heat to 325°F (170°C) Gas 3 and bake for further 25–30 minutes. Serve hot or cold with salad and potatoes.

Onion flan

Overall timing 2¼ hours

Freezing Suitable: reheat from frozen in 350°F (180°C) Gas 4 oven for 20 minutes

To serve 4–6

1 teasp	Dried yeast	5 ml
	Pinch of sugar	
4 fl oz	Lukewarm water	120 ml
8 oz	Plain flour	225 g
1 teasp	Salt	5 ml
1	Egg	1
Filling		
5 oz	Bacon rashers	150 g
6 oz	Onions	175 g
1 oz	Butter	25 g
5 oz	Cheddar cheese	150 g

Mix yeast and sugar with most of the water and leave in a warm place for 15 minutes till frothy.

Sift flour and salt into bowl, make a well in the centre and add yeast mixture, any remaining water and egg. Mix well to a dough, then turn on to floured surface and knead for 5 minutes until smooth and elastic. Place dough in a clean bowl, cover with a damp cloth and leave to rise in a warm place for 45 minutes–1 hour, until doubled in size.

Preheat oven to 400°F (200°C) Gas 6.

Roll out dough on a floured surface and use to line a greased 10 inch (25 cm) loose-bottomed flan tin. Prove for 15 minutes.

Derind and chop bacon. Peel onions and cut into rings. Melt butter in a pan and fry onions for 5 minutes till golden. Slice the cheese.

Cover flan base with onions and bacon and arrange cheese slices on top. Bake for 30–35 minutes. Remove from tin and serve hot.

Storecupboard pizza

Overall timing 1 hour 10 minutes

Freezing Suitable: reheat from frozen in 400°F (200°C) Gas 6 oven for 40 minutes

To serve 4–6

14 oz	Can of tomatoes	396 g
2	Garlic cloves	2
1	Small onion	1
½ teasp	Dried basil	2.5 ml
	Salt and pepper	
4 oz	Can of sardines	125 g
6 oz	Cheddar cheese	175 g
1	Can of anchovy fillets	1
12	Small black olives	12
2 tbsp	Grated Parmesan cheese	2x15 ml
Base		
8 oz	Self-raising flour	225 g
	Pinch of salt	
3 tbsp	Oil	3x15 ml

Preheat oven to 450°F (230°C) Gas 8.

Mix together mashed tomatoes and juice, crushed garlic, chopped onion, herbs, seasoning and drained and chopped sardines. Leave for 15 minutes.

Meanwhile, for the base, sift flour and salt into a bowl. Stir in oil and sufficient water to mix to a soft dough. Roll out dough to a large round and place on a greased baking tray. Pinch up edge to make a ridge. Brush with oil.

Spread tomato mixture over base. Cover with grated or sliced Cheddar and arrange anchovy fillets in a lattice shape on top. Garnish with olives and sprinkle with Parmesan.

Bake for 15 minutes. Reduce heat to 375°F (190°C) Gas 5 and bake for a further 20–25 minutes.

Asparagus quiche

Overall timing 1¼ hours

Freezing Suitable: thaw and refresh in hot oven for 10 minutes

To serve 4

8 oz	Shortcrust pastry	225 g
2 tbsp	Butter	2x15 ml
4 tbsp	Plain flour	4x15 ml
¾ pint	Milk	400 ml
	Salt and pepper	
	Pinch of grated nutmeg	
2	Eggs	2
4 oz	Mature cheese	125 g
12 oz	Can of asparagus	340 g

Preheat the oven to 425°F (220°C) Gas 7.

Roll out the dough to ¼ inch (6 mm) thick and use to line greased 10 inch (25 cm) flan ring or dish. Prick with fork. Bake blind for 5 minutes.

Melt the butter in a small saucepan. Stir in flour. Gradually stir in ½ pint (300 ml) of the milk. Season with salt, pepper and nutmeg. Bring to the boil, stirring constantly. Cook for 2 minutes. Remove pan from heat. Separate the eggs and stir one yolk into sauce. Grate the cheese and add to the sauce.

Pour the sauce into the flan case. Return to the oven and bake for 15 minutes.

Remove quiche from oven. Reduce heat to 375°F (190°C) Gas 5. Drain asparagus, cut into small lengths and arrange evenly over surface. Mix together the rest of the milk, the remaining egg yolk and 2 egg whites and pour this over top. Bake for 30 minutes more.

Leek and bacon bake

Overall timing 50 minutes

Freezing Not suitable

To serve 4

2 lb	Potatoes	900 g
	Salt and pepper	
8 oz	Thick rashers of back bacon	225 g
1 lb	Leeks	450 g
2 oz	Butter	50 g
$\frac{1}{4}$ pint	Milk	150 ml
2	Eggs	2
$\frac{1}{4}$ teasp	Grated nutmeg	1.25 ml
1 tbsp	Chopped parsley	15 ml

Preheat the oven to 375°F (190°C) Gas 5.

Peel potatoes and cook in boiling salted water for 15–20 minutes till tender.

Meanwhile, derind and dice bacon. Trim and thinly slice leeks. Melt the butter in a frying pan and fry the bacon and leeks until golden.

Drain and mash the potatoes with the milk. Add the bacon and leeks with the butter they were cooked in. Beat in the eggs, nutmeg, parsley and seasoning.

Pour into a greased ovenproof dish and bake for 20 minutes till lightly set and golden. Serve immediately.

Vegetable-stuffed tomatoes

Overall timing 50 minutes

Freezing Not suitable

To serve 4

4	Large tomatoes	4
1½ lb	Fresh peas	700 g
1	Onion	1
2 tbsp	Oil	2x15 ml
	Salt and pepper	
2 oz	Butter	50 g
3 tbsp	Plain flour	3x15 ml
½ pint	Milk	300 ml
4 oz	Cheese	125 g
1 tbsp	Fresh breadcrumbs	15 ml

Preheat the oven to 400°F (200°C) Gas 6.

Halve the tomatoes and scoop out the flesh. Discard the seeds and chop the flesh. Shell the peas. Peel and finely chop the onion.

Heat the oil in a frying pan and fry the onion till transparent. Add the peas, cover and cook for 5 minutes. Stir in the chopped tomato flesh, season and continue cooking, covered, for 10 minutes.

Meanwhile, melt the butter in a saucepan. Stir in the flour and cook for 1 minute. Gradually stir in the milk and bring to the boil, stirring until thickened.

Grate the cheese. Mix three-quarters into the sauce with the pea mixture. Use to fill the tomato halves and arrange in an ovenproof dish. Mix the remaining cheese with the breadcrumbs and sprinkle over the tomatoes. Bake for 20 minutes and serve hot.

Romanian peppers

Overall timing 1¼ hours

Freezing Not suitable

To serve 6

1 lb	Lean pork	450 g
2	Onions	2
2 oz	Butter	50 g
4 oz	Button mushrooms	125 g
8 oz	Tomatoes	225 g
½ pint	Water	300 ml
	Salt and pepper	
½ teasp	Paprika	2.5 ml
6	Green peppers	6
2 teasp	Cornflour	2x5 ml
4 tbsp	Top of milk	4x15 ml
	Tabasco sauce	

Dice the pork. Peel and finely chop onions. Melt butter in saucepan. Fry onions and pork for 10 minutes.

Slice mushrooms. Blanch, peel and chop tomatoes. Add mushrooms and tomatoes to the saucepan. Pour in water and cook for 40 minutes over a low heat. Season with salt, pepper and paprika.

Cut tops off peppers. Remove seeds. Place peppers and their tops in a saucepan of boiling water and cook for 5 minutes or until just soft. Lift out and drain. Keep warm.

Blend cornflour with top of milk. Stir into pork mixture, then bring just to the boil to thicken. Season with a few drops of Tabasco sauce. Mix well, then use mixture to fill peppers. Place tops on peppers to serve.

Scalloped Chinese leaves

Overall timing 45 minutes

Freezing Not suitable

To serve 4

2 lb	Chinese leaves	900 g
1	Onion	1
1 pint	Milk	560 ml
	Salt and pepper	
1	Egg	1
2 tbsp	Chopped parsley	2x15 ml
1 oz	Butter	25 g
4 oz	Cheese	125 g

Preheat the oven to 375°F (190°C) Gas 5.

Trim stalk end of Chinese leaves. Remove any damaged outer leaves, then separate remaining leaves. Rinse and drain.

Peel and slice the onion and put into a large saucepan with the milk and a little salt. Bring just to boil, then add the Chinese leaves. Cover and simmer for 5 minutes.

Lift the Chinese leaves out of the milk with a draining spoon and arrange in a shallow ovenproof dish. Beat the egg in a bowl with the parsley and gradually add the milk, beating constantly. Add pepper and the butter and stir till melted. Pour over the Chinese leaves. Grate the cheese and sprinkle over the top. Bake for about 30 minutes till golden. Serve immediately with brown bread rolls.

Bubble and squeak

Overall timing 15 minutes

Freezing Not suitable

To serve 4-6

1 lb	Mashed potatoes	450 g
1 lb	Cooked shredded cabbage	450 g
	Salt and pepper	
1 lb	Leftover cooked meat	450 g
2 oz	Butter	50 g

Beat together mashed potatoes and cabbage with a wooden spoon, adding plenty of seasoning. Dice meat.

Melt the butter in a heavy frying pan and add the potato and cabbage mixture, spreading it over the bottom of the pan. Mix in meat. Fry, turning the mixture occasionally, until crisp and golden brown. Serve immediately.

Leeks with mustard sauce

Overall timing 30 minutes

Freezing Not suitable

To serve 4–6

2 lb	Leeks	900 g
	Salt and pepper	
4 oz	Cheese	125 g
1	Small onion	1
1	Garlic clove	1
2 oz	Butter	50 g
2 tbsp	Plain flour	2x15 ml
$\frac{3}{4}$ pint	Milk	400 ml
1 tbsp	Made mustard	15 ml

Trim leeks. Cook in boiling salted water for 15–20 minutes till tender. Drain, saving $\frac{1}{4}$ pint (150 ml) cooking liquor. Arrange leeks in warmed serving dish. Keep hot.

Grate cheese. Peel and chop onion and garlic. Melt the butter in a saucepan and fry the onion and garlic till golden. Stir in the flour and cook for 1 minute. Gradually add reserved cooking liquor and milk. Bring to the boil, stirring, and cook for 3 minutes. Stir in mustard, cheese and seasoning and heat through gently without boiling. Pour over leeks and serve immediately.

Potato gnocchi

Overall timing 1½ hours plus chilling

Freezing Not suitable

To serve 6

2 lb	Floury potatoes	900 g
	Salt and pepper	
8 oz	Plain flour	225 g
1 teasp	Baking powder	5 ml
2	Eggs	2
6 oz	Slices of cheese	175 g
2 oz	Butter	50 g
3 tbsp	Grated Parmesan cheese	3x15 ml

Scrub the potatoes and cook in boiling salted water for about 30 minutes till tender. Drain, peel and press through a sieve into a large bowl.

Sift the flour and baking powder together, add to the potatoes and mix in with a wooden spoon. Beat in the eggs and seasoning. Spread out on a plate and chill for 2–3 hours till firm.

Preheat oven to 425°F (220°C) Gas 7.

Bring a large pan of salted water to the boil, then reduce heat till simmering. Put teaspoonfuls of the potato mixture into the water and cook for about 4 minutes or till they rise to the surface. Remove with a draining spoon and keep hot while you cook the rest.

Layer cooked dumplings in an ovenproof dish with slices of cheese and butter and sprinkle Parmesan on top. Brown in the oven for 5–10 minutes.

Spring vegetable pie

Overall timing 2 hours

Freezing Not suitable

To serve 6

1 lb	Spring greens	450 g
2	Small globe artichokes	2
1½ lb	Fresh peas	700 g
	Salt and pepper	
1	Large onion	1
3 oz	Butter	75 g
8 oz	Shortcrust pastry	225 g
4	Eggs	4
4 tbsp	Grated Parmesan cheese	4x15 ml
1 tbsp	Chopped parsley	15 ml

Pick over the spring greens, discarding any damaged parts, and chop coarsely. Remove stems and tough outer leaves from artichokes and cut artichokes into quarters, discarding the hairy chokes. Shell peas. Bring a pan of lightly salted water to the boil, add the artichokes and peas and simmer for 10 minutes.

Peel and chop onion. Melt butter in large saucepan, add onion and fry till golden.

Drain artichokes and peas and add to the onion with the spring greens and seasoning. Mix well, cover tightly and simmer for 10 minutes, shaking the pan occasionally. Cool.

Preheat oven to 400°F (200°C) Gas 6.

Roll out two-thirds of dough and use to line an 8 inch (20cm) springform tin. Spread vegetables in tin. Beat three of the eggs lightly with cheese and parsley, then pour over vegetables. Roll out remaining dough and cover filling. Beat remaining egg and brush over pie. Place tin on a baking tray and bake for 30 minutes.

Remove sides of tin. Brush sides of pie with egg and bake for a further 10–15 minutes till golden.

Stuffed cabbage

Overall timing 2 hours 10 minutes

Freezing Not suitable

To serve 6

8 oz	Streaky bacon	225 g
2	Onions	2
2 tbsp	Oil	2x15 ml
1	Green cabbage	1
2	Tomatoes	2
1	Garlic clove	1
1¾ lb	Sausagemeat	750 g
4 oz	Rice	125 g
4 oz	Frozen peas	125 g
	Salt and pepper	
1¾ pints	Hot beef stock	1 litre

Derind and chop bacon. Peel and finely chop onions. Heat oil in frying pan. Add bacon and cook till crisp. Add onions and cook gently for 10 minutes.

Remove all large outer leaves of cabbage. On a large piece of muslin make two layers of leaves in a circular shape. Finely chop remaining cabbage.

Finely chop tomatoes. Peel and crush garlic. Add tomatoes and garlic to chopped cabbage with sausagemeat, rice, peas, bacon and onion and seasoning. Mix well and form into a ball. Place in centre of cabbage leaves, then remake cabbage shape so leaves cover stuffing. Lift corners of muslin and tie at top. Place cabbage in stock, cover and simmer for 1½ hours.

Breton beans

Overall timing 1½ hours

Freezing Suitable

To serve 4-6

8 oz	Dried butter beans	225 g
2	Onions	2
2	Cloves	2
1	Carrot	1
1	Garlic clove	1
¼ teasp	Dried mixed herbs	1.25 ml
2	Bay leaves	2
	Salt and pepper	
1 lb	Tomatoes	450 g
2 oz	Butter	50 g

Place beans in a saucepan, cover with water and simmer for 15 minutes.

Peel one onion and spike with cloves; peel and slice carrot. Peel and crush garlic. Drain beans and return to pan. Add onion, carrot, garlic and herbs. Cover with water and bring to the boil. Cover and cook for 50 minutes; add salt and cook for another 20.

Meanwhile, peel and chop remaining onions. Blanch, peel and quarter tomatoes. Melt butter in a saucepan and add onions, tomatoes and seasoning. Simmer for 20 minutes.

Drain beans and mix into tomato sauce.

Potato cake

Overall timing 50 minutes

Freezing Not suitable

To serve 4

2 lb	Potatoes	900 g
6 oz	Cheese	175 g
3	Eggs	3
½ pint	Milk	300 ml
	Salt and pepper	

Preheat the oven to 375°F (190°C) Gas 5.

Peel potatoes and grate into bowl. Grate cheese and add to potatoes. Beat in eggs, milk and seasoning. Pour into an ovenproof dish and bake for 40 minutes till top is golden. Serve hot.

Potato omelette

Overall timing 30 minutes

Freezing Not suitable

To serve 4

4x6 oz	Waxy potatoes	4x175 g
	Salt and pepper	
8 oz	Butter	225 g
2	Sage leaves	2
12	Eggs	12

Peel and dice the potatoes. Cook in boiling salted water for 4 minutes. Drain and pat dry.

Melt 2 oz (50 g) of the butter in a frying pan, add the potatoes and sage and fry over a moderate heat for 5–10 minutes till the potatoes are tender and golden. Discard sage leaves, remove potatoes and keep hot.

Lightly beat three of the eggs in a bowl with salt and pepper. Heat omelette pan and add one-quarter of the remaining butter. Pour eggs into pan and cook omelette. When almost set, put one-quarter of the potatoes along the centre and fold the sides in to cover them. Turn on to a warm plate with the join down and keep hot while you cook the remaining three omelettes.

Just before serving, cut along the tops of the omelettes to expose the filling. Serve immediately with a mixed salad.

Stuffed squash or marrow

Overall timing 1 hour

Freezing Not suitable

To serve 4

4	Small squash or marrows	4
	Salt and pepper	
1	Large onion	1
1 tbsp	Oil	15 ml
12 oz	Minced beef	350 g
8 oz	Sausagemeat	225 g
1 tbsp	Plain flour	15 ml
¼ pint	Stock	150 ml
1 tbsp	Tomato purée	15 ml
2 oz	Fresh breadcrumbs	50 g
1 tbsp	Chopped parsley	15 ml
1 oz	Butter	25 g

Preheat the oven to 400°F (200°C) Gas 6.

Blanch the squash or marrows in boiling salted water for 10 minutes.

Meanwhile, peel and finely chop the onion. Heat the oil in a saucepan, add the onion and fry till transparent. Add the minced beef and sausagemeat and fry, stirring to break up the meat. Sprinkle in the flour and fry gently for 5 minutes till browned.

Drain the squash or marrows. Cut a lid from the top of each, scoop out the seeds and discard. Scoop out and reserve some of the flesh, leaving a shell about ½ inch (12.5 mm) thick. Arrange squash in a shallow ovenproof dish.

Gradually add stock to meat mixture and bring to the boil, stirring. Chop the flesh from the squash and add to the pan with the tomato purée and seasoning. Cover and simmer for 10 minutes.

Add breadcrumbs and parsley to meat mixture and mix well. Divide between the squash, pressing it in firmly. Replace lids. Brush squash with melted butter, then bake for 20 minutes till tender. Serve immediately with a tossed green salad and rye bread.

Bacon and cabbage casserole

Overall timing 1¼ hours

Freezing Not suitable

To serve 4

1	Medium-size white cabbage	1
2	Onions	2
1 oz	Lard	25 g
8 oz	Back bacon	225 g
1 lb	Minced beef	450 g
1 teasp	Caraway seeds	5 ml
¼ pint	Beef stock	150 ml
	Salt and pepper	
2 oz	Butter	50 g
8 oz	Streaky bacon rashers	225 g

Preheat the oven to 375°F (190°C) Gas 5.

Discard any marked outer leaves of the cabbage. Save two or three good ones. Cut the remaining cabbage in half. Remove the core, then shred the cabbage. Put with reserved leaves into a saucepan of cold water. Bring to the boil and drain. Set aside.

Peel and chop the onions. Melt the lard in a large saucepan, add the onions and cook gently for 3–4 minutes. Derind and chop back bacon. Add to the saucepan. Cook for 2–3 minutes. Add the minced beef and cook, stirring, until brown. Add the caraway seeds, stock and seasoning. Simmer for 10 minutes.

Melt the butter in a small saucepan. Put half of the shredded cabbage in the bottom of an ovenproof dish and pour the melted butter over. Spread the mince mixture evenly over the cabbage. Cover with remaining shredded cabbage and top with whole leaves. Arrange the streaky bacon rashers over the top of the cabbage. Bake for 45 minutes.

Savoury pumpkin

Overall timing 1¼ hours plus 30 minutes standing

Freezing Not suitable

To serve 4–6

2 lb	Pumpkin	900 g
	Salt and pepper	
8 oz	Cheese	225 g
¼ teasp	Ground cumin	1.25 ml
3	Eggs	3
2 oz	Fresh breadcrumbs	50 g
2 tbsp	Chopped parsley	2 x 15 ml
1 oz	Butter	25 g

Scrape the seeds and fibrous centre out of the pumpkin. Remove the skin and grate the flesh into a bowl. Sprinkle with salt, mix well and leave to stand for 30 minutes.

Preheat the oven to 350°F (180°C) Gas 4.

Press the pumpkin with the back of a spoon to squeeze out as much liquid as possible. Grate the cheese and add to the pumpkin with cumin, eggs, breadcrumbs, parsley and seasoning and beat the mixture till smooth.

Pour into a greased ovenproof dish and smooth the top. Dot with butter and bake for about 45 minutes till set. Serve immediately with a tomato salad and fresh crusty bread and butter.

Cauliflower ring

Overall timing 1¼ hours

Freezing Not suitable

To serve 4–6

1	Large cauliflower	1
	Salt and pepper	
4 oz	Butter	125 g
2 oz	Plain flour	50 g
¾ pint	Milk	400 ml
¼ teasp	Grated nutmeg	1.25 ml
4 oz	Gruyère or Cheddar cheese	125 g
3	Eggs	3
1 tbsp	Dried breadcrumbs	15 ml
	Sprigs of parsley	

Preheat oven to 375°F (190°C) Gas 5.

Trim cauliflower and divide into florets. Cook for 7–10 minutes in boiling salted water. Drain, chop and put in bowl.

To make sauce, melt 2 oz (50 g) of the butter in a pan, stir in flour and cook for 1 minute. Gradually stir in milk. Bring to the boil, stirring, and cook for 1 minute. Add seasoning and nutmeg. Grate cheese and stir 3 oz (75 g) into sauce.

Remove pan from heat. Pour about two-thirds of the sauce into a bowl and set aside. Stir eggs into sauce left in pan. Mix sauce thoroughly into cauliflower.

Grease a 9½ inch (24 cm) ring mould with half remaining butter. Sprinkle breadcrumbs on bottom. Fill with cauliflower mixture, pressing down well, and bake for 30–35 minutes.

Remove from oven and immerse mould up to rim in cold water. Turn up oven to 450°F (230°C) Gas 8. Run a knife blade around the sides of the mould, then carefully turn out on to ovenproof dish (if any of the mixture sticks to mould, quickly smooth it back into position with a knife and a little of remaining sauce).

Spread reserved sauce over cauliflower ring and sprinkle with remaining cheese. Melt remaining 1 oz (25 g) butter and pour over. Return to oven and bake for about 15 minutes until golden brown. Serve hot.

Vegetable croquettes

Overall timing 1¼ hours plus chilling

Freezing Suitable: deep fry after thawing

To serve 4

1½ lb	Floury potatoes	700 g
1	Large parsnip	1
	Salt and pepper	
2	Large leeks	2
1	Stalk of celery	1
2	Large carrots	2
2 oz	Butter	50 g
2 tbsp	Chopped parsley	2x15 ml
¼ teasp	Grated nutmeg	1.25 ml
2	Eggs	2
	Oil for deep frying	
4 tbsp	Plain flour	4x15 ml
	Sprigs of parsley	

Peel and chop the potatoes and parsnip. Cook in boiling salted water for 15–20 minutes till tender.

Meanwhile, trim and finely shred leeks and celery. Peel and grate carrots. Melt butter in a frying pan, add leeks and celery and fry till golden.

Drain potatoes and parsnip, return to pan and shake over a low heat to dry throughly. Remove from heat and mash to a smooth purée. Stir in fried vegetables and any pan juices. Add carrots, parsley, nutmeg and seasoning. Beat in eggs. Spread the mixture on a plate, cool, then chill for 2–3 hours till firm.

Heat oil in a deep-fryer to 340°F (170°C). Shape vegetable mixture into 20 balls with floured hands. Fry, a few at a time, for 5–6 minutes, till crisp and golden. Drain on kitchen paper. Serve hot, garnished with parsley.

Casseroled lettuce rolls

Overall timing 1 hour

Freezing Not suitable

To serve 4

8 oz	Streaky bacon	225 g
10	Large lettuce leaves	10
2	Onions	2
2	Carrots	2
	Salt and pepper	
¼ pint	Stock	150 ml
2 tbsp	Lemon juice	2x15 ml
Stuffing		
1	Onion	1
2 tbsp	Oil	2x15 ml
8 oz	Chicken livers	225 g
2 oz	Long grain rice	50 g
½ pint	Chicken stock	300 ml
	Bouquet garni	
	Salt and pepper	

To make the stuffing, peel and chop onion. Heat oil in pan and fry onion till golden. Chop chicken livers. Add to pan and brown on all sides.

Add rice, stock, bouquet garni and seasoning. Bring to the boil. Cover and simmer for 15 minutes, shaking pan frequently.

Meanwhile, derind and halve bacon rashers, then use them to line bottom and sides of an ovenproof dish. Wash and dry lettuce leaves. Peel and slice onions into rings. Peel and thinly slice carrots. Blanch lettuce, onions and carrots in boiling salted water for 3 minutes. Drain thoroughly.

Preheat the oven to 350°F (180°C) Gas 4.

Spread out lettuce leaves. Taste stuffing and adjust seasoning. Divide between lettuce leaves. Fold in sides of leaves, then roll up tightly round stuffing. Arrange, join side down, in ovenproof dish. Add blanched onions and carrots. Mix stock, lemon juice and seasoning. Pour over lettuce. Cover tightly and bake for 25–30 minutes.

Stuffed cucumbers

Overall timing 1 hour

Freezing Suitable

To serve 6

3	Large cucumbers	3
2oz	Cooked ham	50g
4oz	Minced beef	125g
2 tbsp	Fresh breadcrumbs	2x15ml
1 tbsp	Chopped parsley	15ml
3 tbsp	Milk	3x15ml
1	Egg	1
	Salt and pepper	
Sauce		
1	Onion	1
1	Leek	1
2oz	Butter	50g
1oz	Plain flour	25g
½ pint	Stock	300ml
1 tbsp	Chopped parsley	15ml
	Paprika	
	Salt	
1 tbsp	Vinegar	15ml
4fl oz	Top of milk	120ml

Peel cucumbers. Halve them lengthways and scoop out seeds. Finely chop ham and mix with beef, breadcrumbs, parsley, milk, egg and seasoning. Stuff cucumbers with mixture.

To make sauce, peel and finely chop onion. Trim and finely chop leek. Melt butter in a saucepan and fry onion and leek till golden. Sprinkle flour into pan and cook for 1 minute, stirring. Gradually stir in stock, then add parsley, a pinch each of paprika and salt and the vinegar. Bring to the boil, stirring.

Arrange cucumbers on top of sauce and surround with any leftover stuffing. Cover and cook gently for 30 minutes. Turn cucumbers over halfway through cooking time.

Stir milk into sauce and heat through uncovered for 2 minutes.

Leek and cheese soufflé

Overall timing 1 hour

Freezing Not suitable

To serve 4

2 oz	Butter	50 g
2 oz	Plain flour	50 g
$\frac{1}{4}$ pint	Warm milk	300 ml
2 oz	Red Leicester cheese	50 g
8 oz	Leeks	225 g
	Salt and pepper	
3	Large eggs	3

Melt the butter in a pan, stir in the flour and cook for 1 minute. Gradually add warm milk and bring to the boil, stirring. Simmer for 2 minutes. Remove from heat and leave to cool.

Grate the cheese. Trim and finely chop leeks. Blanch in boiling water for 5 minutes and drain thoroughly. Stir the grated cheese and leeks into sauce and season. Separate eggs. Beat the yolks into the sauce.

Whisk egg whites in a bowl till stiff but not dry. Stir 1 tbsp (15 ml) whisked whites into sauce to lighten it, then carefully fold in the rest. Turn mixture into greased 2 pint (1.1 litre) soufflé dish, place on baking tray and bake for 30–35 minutes till well risen and golden. Serve immediately.

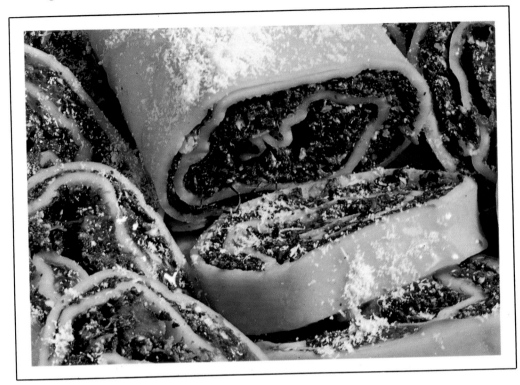

Cottage spinach roll

Overall timing 1¾ hours

Freezing Not suitable

To serve 4–6

8 oz	Plain flour	225 g
	Salt and pepper	
2	Eggs	2
2 lb	Spinach	900 g
3 oz	Butter	75 g
8 oz	Cottage cheese	225 g
¼ teasp	Grated nutmeg	1.25 ml
6 tbsp	Grated Parmesan cheese	6x15 ml

Sift the flour and ½ teasp (2.5 ml) salt into a bowl. Beat the eggs lightly in a bowl, pour half into the flour and mix with a palette knife. Add enough of the remaining egg to make a stiff dough. Knead till smooth, then chill for 30 minutes.

Meanwhile, wash and pick over the spinach. Put into a saucepan with only the water that clings to it. Cover and cook gently for 5 minutes. Drain thoroughly, then shred.

Melt 1 oz (25 g) of the butter in a frying pan, add the spinach and cook for 5 minutes, stirring occasionally. Pour into a bowl and add the cottage cheese, nutmeg, half the Parmesan and seasoning. Mix well. Leave to cool.

Roll out the dough on a floured surface to a rectangle about 15x12 inches (38x30 cm). With a long side nearest you, spread the filling over the dough, leaving a 1 inch (2.5 cm) border. Fold the bottom border over the filling and roll up. Pinch the ends together to seal.

Wrap the roll in a double thickness of muslin, tying the ends with string. Place in a large pan of boiling salted water, cover and simmer for 25 minutes.

Drain and unwrap the roll and place on a warmed serving dish. Melt the remaining butter. Cut the roll into thick slices, pour the butter over and sprinkle with the remaining Parmesan. Serve immediately.

Alsace onion mould

Overall timing 1½ hours

Freezing Not suitable

To serve 6

1½ lb	Onions	700 g
3 oz	Butter	75 g
4 tbsp	Plain flour	4x15 ml
¼ pint	Carton of single cream or top of milk	150 ml
2	Eggs	2
¼ teasp	Grated nutmeg	1.25 ml
	Salt and pepper	

Preheat the oven to 425°F (220°C) Gas 7. Grease a 5 inch (13 cm) mould or cake tin and put in the oven for 10 minutes to heat up.

Peel and thinly slice the onions. Melt the butter in a saucepan and add the onions. Cook till transparent.

Add the flour and cook, stirring, for 2 minutes. Gradually add the cream or top of milk and bring to the boil, stirring constantly. Cook for 2 minutes till thick. Remove from the heat and beat in the eggs and nutmeg. Season to taste. Pour into the hot mould or tin.

Bake for about 45 minutes till lightly set and golden. Run a knife around the edge of the mould and turn out on to a warmed serving dish. Serve immediately, cut into wedges. Provide a pepper mill, so everyone can add as they wish.

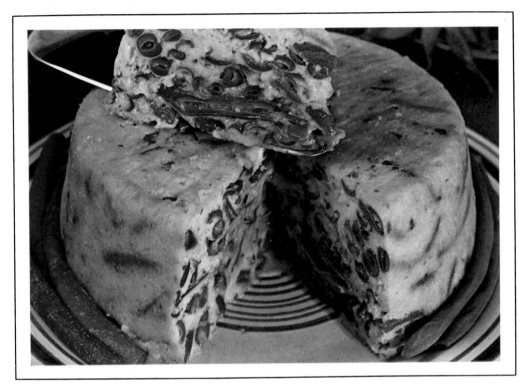

Bean cake

Overall timing 1¼–1½ hours

Freezing Suitable: reheat after thawing in 300°F (150°C) Gas 2 oven for 30 minutes

To serve 4

1 lb	Green beans	450 g
	Salt and pepper	
1	Celery stalk	1
3 oz	Butter	75 g
2 tbsp	Oil	2x15 ml
1 tbsp	Chopped onion	15 ml
1 tbsp	Chopped parsley	15 ml
1 oz	Plain flour	25 g
9 fl oz	Milk	250 ml
4 oz	Mature cheese	125 g
2 tbsp	Crisp breadcrumbs	2x15 ml
3	Eggs	3

Preheat the oven to 425°F (220°C) Gas 7.

String beans. Blanch for 5 minutes in boiling salted water. Drain.

Chop celery. Melt 2 oz (50 g) of the butter with the oil in a frying pan and brown the onion, celery and chopped parsley. Add beans, cover and cook very gently for 10 minutes.

Meanwhile, melt the remaining butter in a saucepan. Stir in flour and cook for 2 minutes, then gradually stir in milk. Simmer until thick. Grate cheese and add to sauce with seasoning.

Grease ovenproof dish and coat bottom and sides with breadcrumbs. Drain bean mixture and mix it into sauce until well combined, then mix in lightly beaten eggs. Spoon mixture into dish. Place dish in roasting tin of water and bake for 25 minutes. Reduce heat to 400°F (200°C) Gas 6 and bake for 10 more minutes.

Remove dish from oven, leave to stand for 5 minutes, then invert on to serving plate. Serve hot or cold.

Lentil risotto

Overall timing 1 hour

Freezing Not suitable

To serve 6

8 oz	Continental lentils	225 g
1	Onion	1
4 oz	Butter	125 g
	Salt and pepper	
12 oz	Long grain rice	350 g
2 pints	Stock	1.1 litres
2 oz	Grated Parmesan cheese	50 g

Wash and pick over lentils. Peel and finely chop the onion. Melt the butter in a large saucepan, add the onion and cook till transparent. Add the lentils and enough water to cover. Season and bring to the boil. Reduce heat, cover and simmer for 1 hour.

Add the rice and stock. Bring back to the boil, reduce heat, cover and simmer for a further 15–18 minutes or until rice is just tender.

Stir in the Parmesan, and taste and adjust seasoning. Serve hot.

Pipérade

Overall timing 1 hour

Freezing Not suitable

To serve 4

1 lb	Ripe tomatoes	450 g
2	Green peppers	2
2	Onions	2
1	Garlic clove	1
5 tbsp	Oil	5x15 ml
	Salt and pepper	
$\frac{1}{4}$ teasp	Dried marjoram	1.25 ml
	Tabasco sauce	
8	Eggs	8

Blanch, peel and chop tomatoes. Deseed and chop peppers. Peel and slice onions. Peel and crush garlic.

Heat oil in frying pan. Add onions and garlic and cook till golden. Add peppers and tomatoes and cook over a high heat for 5 minutes. Season with salt, pepper, marjoram and Tabasco. Reduce heat, cover and simmer for 30 minutes or until the mixture is reduced to a purée.

Lightly beat eggs in a bowl. Season and pour over vegetable purée. Cook over increased heat, stirring, for 2–3 minutes till creamy. Serve with buttered toast and a green salad.

Curried eggs

Overall timing 35 minutes

Freezing Not suitable

To serve 4

6	Eggs	6
2	Onions	2
2 oz	Butter	50 g
2 teasp	Curry powder	2x5 ml
1 pint	Chicken stock	560 ml
1 teasp	Cornflour	5 ml
4 fl oz	Carton of single cream or top of milk	120 ml
	Salt and pepper	

Place eggs in a saucepan of cold water. Bring to the boil and simmer for 8 minutes, then drain.

Peel and finely chop onions. Melt butter in a frying pan, add onions, cover and cook until golden over a low heat (about 15 minutes).

Sprinkle with curry powder and cook for 2 minutes, stirring. Pour in the stock and simmer for 10 minutes. Mix cornflour and cream or milk together well, then stir into curry mixture with seasoning. Heat gently but do not boil.

Shell eggs and cut in half lengthways. Remove yolks with a spoon and mash yolks and a little of the curry mixture together with a fork. Spoon back into egg whites. Place eggs in curry sauce and heat through without boiling. Serve with rice or hot buttered toast.

Eggs florentine

Overall timing 45 minutes

Freezing Not suitable

To serve 4

2 lb	Spinach	900 g
2 oz	Butter	50 g
	Salt	
$\frac{1}{4}$ teasp	Grated nutmeg	1.25 ml
$1\frac{1}{2}$ oz	Plain flour	40 g
$\frac{3}{4}$ pint	Milk	400 ml
3 oz	Cheese	75 g
	Cayenne pepper	
$\frac{1}{2}$ teasp	Made mustard	2.5 ml
8	Hard-boiled eggs	8
2 tbsp	Fresh white breadcrumbs	2x15 ml

Preheat the oven to 425°F (220°C) Gas 7.

Wash spinach well in several changes of water. Remove any coarse stalks. Put into saucepan with only the water that still clings to the spinach after washing. Cook for 5–10 minutes till tender. Stir in $\frac{1}{2}$ oz (15 g) of the butter and season with salt and grated nutmeg, then spread over the bottom of a greased ovenproof dish.

Melt remaining butter in a pan. Stir in the flour and cook for 1 minute. Gradually add the milk, bring to the boil, stirring, and cook for 2 minutes.

Grate cheese. Reserve 2 tbsp (2x15 ml) for the topping and stir the rest into the sauce with a pinch each of salt and cayenne and the mustard.

Shell eggs and arrange on top of spinach. Pour sauce over eggs. Mix reserved grated cheese and breadcrumbs and sprinkle over the top. Bake for 10 minutes till cheese is bubbly and golden. Serve immediately.

Tomatoes and eggs American style

Overall timing 20 minutes

Freezing Not suitable

To serve 4–6

8 oz	Streaky bacon rashers	225 g
6	Large tomatoes	6
½ pint	Milk	300 ml
	Salt and pepper	
6	Eggs	6

Preheat the grill. Derind the bacon and arrange on the grill pan. Grill till crisp and golden. Remove and keep hot.

Wipe the tomatoes and cut in half. Place the tomatoes cut sides down on the grill pan and brush with a little fat from the bacon. Grill about 3 inches (7.5 cm) below heat for 3–4 minutes.

Meanwhile, pour the milk into a frying pan, add a pinch of salt and heat till simmering. Break an egg on to a saucer, then slide it into the milk. Repeat with remaining eggs. Cover and poach for 3 minutes.

Turn the tomatoes over, brush with bacon fat and grill for 2 more minutes. Arrange stalk halves cut sides up in a warmed serving dish and season. Lift the eggs out of the milk with a draining spoon and drain on kitchen paper. Place one on each tomato half and cover with the remaining halves. Arrange the bacon round the tomatoes and serve immediately with plenty of hot buttered toast.

Snow eggs

Overall timing 40 minutes plus chilling

Freezing Not suitable

To serve 4-6

1 pint	Milk	560 ml
1	Vanilla pod	1
5	Eggs	5
	Pinch of salt	
5 oz	Caster sugar	150 g
2 oz	Icing sugar	50 g
2 tbsp	Water	2x15 ml

Slowly heat the milk in a saucepan with the vanilla pod. Separate the eggs. Mix egg yolks, salt and 3 oz (75 g) of the caster sugar in a bowl. Remove pod and mix milk into eggs.

Return to pan and, stirring constantly, slowly bring to just below boiling point – the mixture will lightly coat the spoon. Do not boil. Remove custard from heat and allow to cool slightly before pouring into serving bowl. Chill.

Heat a saucepan of water. Whisk egg whites till stiff, sprinkle with icing sugar and whisk well again until stiff. Using two soup spoons, make egg shapes of the egg white. Carefully lower a few at a time on to the simmering water and leave for 15 seconds on one side, 10 seconds on the other. Remove egg shapes from pan with a draining spoon and place on a wire rack. Do not let them touch. When all are cooked and dried, carefully place the egg shapes on the custard.

Dissolve remaining sugar in water in a small saucepan and boil till it turns to caramel. Pour over the egg shapes and serve immediately.

Cider and grape ring

Overall timing 15 minutes plus setting

Freezing Not suitable

To serve 4–6

1 pint	Medium-sweet cider	600 ml
1 tbsp	Powdered gelatine	15 ml
1 tbsp	Lemon juice	15 ml
8 oz	White grapes	225 g
8 oz	Black grapes	225 g
2 tbsp	Caster sugar	2x15 ml

Put 6 tbsp (6x15 ml) of the cider in a heatproof bowl, sprinkle over the gelatine and leave until spongy – about 5 minutes.

Dissolve gelatine over a pan of hot water, then stir in the remaining cider and lemon juice. Remove bowl from the heat. Spoon enough of the cider jelly into a dampened 1½ pint (850 ml) ring mould just to cover it. Leave it to set in the refrigerator.

Reserve half of each kind of grape. Wash and cut remainder in half and remove pips. Arrange halves over the set jelly, then cover with more liquid jelly and leave to set. Continue layers, ending with jelly, then chill in refrigerator till set. Wash remaining grapes and remove most of moisture. Toss in caster sugar.

Dip the mould quickly in and out of hot water and invert over a serving plate so jelly slides out. Fill centre with sugared grapes. Serve with whipped cream and ginger biscuits.

Marmalade and ginger tart

Overall timing 1¼ hours

Freezing Not suitable

To serve 6–8

8 oz	Plain flour	225 g
1 teasp	Ground ginger	5 ml
4 oz	Butter	125 g
2 tbsp	Caster sugar	2x15 ml
1	Egg yolk	1
8 tbsp	Marmalade	8x15 ml

Sift flour and ginger into a bowl. Rub in the butter till the mixture resembles breadcrumbs. Add sugar and mix to a dough with the egg yolk and a little water. Knead lightly till smooth, then chill for 30 minutes.

Preheat the oven to 375°F (190°C) Gas 5.

Roll out about three-quarters of the dough on a floured surface and use to line a 9 inch (23 cm) pie plate or flan tin. Crimp the edges and prick base.

Spread a thick layer of marmalade over the tart base. Roll out the remaining dough and cut into strips with a pastry wheel. Make a lattice over the marmalade filling, pressing the joins to seal. Bake for about 40 minutes, till golden. Remove from tin and serve hot or cold with custard or ice cream.

Pear brown betty

Overall timing 1 hour

Freezing Not suitable

To serve 6–8

2 lb	Ripe pears	900 g
8 oz	Stale breadcrumbs	225 g
4 oz	Caster sugar	125 g
2 oz	Butter	50 g

Preheat the oven to 375°F (190°C) Gas 5.

Peel and halve the pears. Remove the cores and cut flesh into $\frac{1}{4}$ inch (6 mm) slices.

Cover the bottom of a greased 8 inch (20 cm) springform tin with a quarter of the bread-crumbs. Arrange one-third of the pears on top and sprinkle with a little sugar. Repeat the layers till all the ingredients have been used.

Dot with the butter and bake for about 45 minutes till the pears are tender and the top is crisp and golden. Remove from the tin and serve hot or cold with pouring cream or custard.

Redcurrant pudding

Overall timing 1½ hours

Freezing Suitable: reheat from frozen in 350°F (180°C) Gas 4 oven for 1 hour

To serve 6–8

12 oz	Redcurrants	350 g
12	Slices of stale bread	12
2 oz	Butter	50 g
1 pint	Milk	560 ml
1	Vanilla pod	1
2	Eggs	2
6 tbsp	Caster sugar	6 x 15 ml

Wash and drain the redcurrants. Remove the stalks. Remove the crusts from the bread. Spread with butter and cut into triangles.

Sprinkle a few redcurrants over the bottom of a well-greased 3 pint (1.7 litre) ovenproof dish and arrange some of the bread on top. Cover with redcurrants, then a layer of bread. Repeat the layers.

Put the milk and vanilla pod into a saucepan and bring to the boil. Remove from the heat and lift out the vanilla pod. Whisk the eggs with 5 tbsp (5x15 ml) of the sugar till frothy, then pour in the hot milk, whisking continuously. Strain the custard over the redcurrants and bread. Leave to soak for 20 minutes.

Preheat the oven to 375°F (190°C) Gas 5.

Sprinkle the remaining sugar over the pudding and bake for about 40 minutes till golden. Serve immediately.

Nutty apple pudding

Overall timing 50 minutes

Freezing Not suitable

To serve 4–6

1½ lb	Cooking apples	700 g
¼ pint	Water	150 ml
2 oz	Flaked almonds	50 g
2 oz	Sultanas	50 g
7 oz	Wholemeal bread	200 g
4 oz	Demerara sugar	125 g
2 oz	Butter	50 g

Preheat the oven to 425°F (220°C) Gas 7.

Peel and core apples and slice into a saucepan. Add water, almonds and sultanas. Cover and cook over a gentle heat for 10 minutes. Remove from heat.

Crumble the bread into a bowl and mix in half the sugar. Grease an ovenproof dish with some of the butter and spread half the bread mixture over the bottom. Cover with apple mixture, then top with remaining bread. Sprinkle on rest of sugar and dot with remaining butter. Bake for about 20 minutes.

Coffee water ice

Overall timing 2 hours

Freezing See method

To serve 6–8

9 oz	Granulated sugar	250 g
1 tbsp	Vanilla sugar	15 ml
1 pint	Water	560 ml
8 teasp	Instant coffee granules	8x5 ml
½ pint	Carton of whipping cream	300 ml
	Peppermint essence (optional)	

Put granulated and vanilla sugar and water in a saucepan. Stir until sugar has completely dissolved, then bring to the boil and boil for 5 minutes. Skim if necessary. Stir in the coffee granules and remove pan from heat. Allow mixture to cool completely.

Pour coffee mixture through a fine sieve or muslin-lined sieve into a freezer tray. Place in freezer or freezing compartment of refrigerator and leave for about 1 hour or until the mixture forms a granular mass. Do not stir.

In a bowl whip cream till just holding soft peaks, then add a few drops of peppermint essence, if using, to taste. Scrape out contents of freezer tray with a fork and divide ice between chilled serving glasses. Top each glass with peppermint-flavoured cream and serve with biscuits.

Loganberry jelly ring

Overall timing 25 minutes plus chilling

Freezing Suitable

To serve 6

14½ oz	Can of loganberries	411 g
1	Raspberry jelly tablet	1
¼ pint	Carton of whipping cream	150 ml
	Langue de chat biscuits	

Drain loganberries, reserving syrup, and press through a sieve. Make up jelly, using loganberry syrup as part of the required amount of liquid. Stir in sieved fruit and leave to cool and set slightly.

Whip cream and fold into berry mixture, then pour into dampened 1½ pint (850 ml) ring mould. Chill till firm (2–4 hours). Chill serving plate at the same time.

Dip the mould in hot water to loosen, turn out on to chilled serving plate and arrange biscuits in centre of ring just before serving.

Baked apples

Overall timing 35 minutes

Freezing Not suitable

To serve 4

4	Large apples	4
8 tbsp	Jam	8x15 ml
1 oz	Butter	25 g
4 tbsp	Water	4x15 ml
4 tbsp	Caster sugar	4x15 ml

Preheat oven to 375°F (190°C) Gas 5.

Wash, dry and core apples. Place in a greased ovenproof dish and fill each apple with jam. Add small knob of butter to each.

Put water in bottom of dish, then bake for 25 minutes. Serve sprinkled with sugar.

Caramelized grapefruit

Overall timing 20 minutes

Freezing Not suitable

To serve 4

2	Grapefruit	2
1 teasp	Ground cinnamon	5 ml
4 tbsp	Caster sugar	4x15 ml

Preheat the grill.

Cut grapefruit in half. Remove flesh with grapefruit knife, separate segments and discard membranes. Put segments into a bowl. Mix cinnamon with half the sugar and sprinkle over fruit.

Fill grapefruit shells with segments and sprinkle with remaining sugar. Grill for a few minutes till golden brown. Serve hot.

Pineapple fritters

Overall timing 25 minutes

Freezing Not suitable

To serve 6

15½ oz	Can of pineapple rings	439 g
4 oz	Plain flour	125 g
1½ teasp	Caster sugar	7.5 ml
1	Whole egg	1
1 tbsp	Oil	15 ml
4 fl oz	Milk or water	120 ml
2	Egg whites	2
	Oil for frying	
3 tbsp	Icing sugar	3x15 ml

Drain the pineapple rings and dry on kitchen paper.

Sift flour and sugar into bowl. Beat in egg, oil and liquid till smooth. Whisk egg whites till stiff and fold into batter.

Heat oil in a deep-fryer to 340°F (170°C). Spear the pineapple rings on a fork, dip into the batter and carefully lower into the oil. Fry three at a time for 2–3 minutes till crisp and golden. Remove from the pan, drain on kitchen paper and keep hot while remaining fritters are cooked.

Arrange on a warmed serving plate, sift the icing sugar over and serve immediately with whipped cream.

French toast

Overall timing 25 minutes

Freezing Not suitable

To serve 4–6

10	Thin slices of bread	10
½–¾ pint	Milk	300–400 ml
2–3	Eggs	2–3
2 oz	Butter	50 g
2 oz	Caster sugar	50 g
1 teasp	Ground cinnamon (optional)	5 ml

Place bread on a baking tray or Swiss roll tin and pour over the milk. The more stale the bread, the more milk you will need to make the bread spongy. Soak for 10 minutes.

Whisk the eggs in a shallow dish till creamy. Lightly press bread with a fork to remove excess milk.

Melt butter in frying pan (reserve some if you cannot cook all slices at once). Dip bread in egg to coat, add to pan and fry for 3–4 minutes on each side. Sprinkle with caster sugar and cinnamon, if used, and serve immediately, with jam or golden or maple syrup.

Baked bananas

Overall timing 15 minutes

Freezing Not suitable

To serve 4

4	Large ripe bananas	4
2 oz	Butter	50 g
2 teasp	Caster sugar	2x5 ml
2 tbsp	Water	2x15 ml
	Ground cinnamon	

Preheat oven to 425°F (220°C) Gas 7.

Peel the bananas three-quarters of the way down. Fold back the skin to give a petal effect. Place in a greased ovenproof dish and dot each banana with butter. Sprinkle with sugar, water and a little ground cinnamon.

Bake for 10 minutes. Serve immediately with custard or vanilla ice cream.

Viennese sweet semolina

Overall timing 50 minutes

Freezing Not suitable

To serve 4–6

2 oz	Sultanas	50 g
1 pint	Milk	560 ml
1½ oz	Butter	40 g
3 oz	Semolina	75 g
4 tbsp	Caster sugar	4x15 ml

Preheat the oven to 350°F (180°C) Gas 4.

Soak the sultanas in warm water. Put the milk into a saucepan with butter. Heat till warm, then pour in the semolina and bring to the boil, stirring constantly. Simmer for 5 minutes, then stir in all but 1 tbsp (15 ml) of the sugar.

Drain sultanas and mix into semolina. Turn into a greased ovenproof dish and smooth top. Bake for 30 minutes.

Remove dish from oven and increase heat to 400°F (200°C) Gas 6. Mix the semolina with a fork to break it up. Return dish to oven for 5 minutes till mixture is dry and crisp. Turn on to a warmed serving dish, sprinkle with the reserved sugar and serve hot.

Tapioca and caramel mould

Overall timing 1¼ hours

Freezing Not suitable

To serve 6

4 oz	Seed pearl tapioca	125 g
1½ pints	Milk	850 ml
4 tbsp	Caster sugar	4x15 ml
	Grated rind of 1 lemon	
4 oz	Granulated sugar	125 g
1 oz	Butter	25 g
3	Eggs	3

Preheat the oven to 400°F (200°C) Gas 6.

Put the tapioca, milk, caster sugar and lemon rind into a saucepan and bring to the boil, stirring. Simmer for 15 minutes, stirring occasionally with a wooden spoon to prevent the mixture sticking to the pan.

Meanwhile, put the granulated sugar into a saucepan with 2 tbsp (2x15 ml) water and stir over a low heat till the sugar dissolves. Stop stirring and boil steadily till golden brown. Pour into a 7 inch (18 cm) round cake tin, turning so the bottom and sides are coated.

Remove the tapioca from the heat and beat in the butter. Separate the eggs, putting the whites into a large bowl. Beat the yolks into the tapioca, then leave to cool, stirring occasionally.

Whisk the egg whites till stiff but not dry and fold gently into the tapioca with a metal spoon. Pour the mixture into the caramel-lined tin and bake for about 35 minutes till well risen and golden.

Run a knife round the edge of the mould and turn out on to a serving dish. Serve hot or cold with pouring cream.

Tarte Tatin

Overall timing 1¼ hours

Freezing Not suitable

To serve 8–10

7 oz	Frozen puff pastry	212 g
3 oz	Unsalted butter	75 g
3 oz	Caster sugar	75 g
7	Large dessert apples	7

Thaw the pastry. Preheat the oven to 425°F (220°C) Gas 7.

Cut the butter into pieces and put into a 9 inch (23 cm) round cake tin with the sugar. Peel and core the apples; cut six of them in half. Arrange the apple halves on end around the side of the tin and place the whole apple in the centre.

Place the tin over a low heat and heat till the butter melts. Increase the heat and cook, shaking the tin occasionally, till the sugar caramelizes and is golden. Remove from the heat. Brush a little water round the edge of the tin.

Roll out the dough on a floured surface to a 9 inch (23 cm) round and place over the apples. Press down lightly.

Bake for 25–30 minutes till the pastry is well risen and golden brown. Leave to cool in the tin for 5 minutes.

Run a knife round the edge of the tart and turn out on to a serving dish so that the caramelized apples are on top. Serve hot or cold with whipped cream or scoops of vanilla ice cream.

Spicy rhubarb pie

Overall timing 1¾ hours

Freezing Not suitable

To serve 6–8

9 oz	Plain flour	250 g
	Pinch of salt	
¼ teasp	Mixed spice	1.25 ml
½ teasp	Ground cinnamon	2.5 ml
5 oz	Butter	150 g
2 tbsp	Caster sugar	2x15 ml
2 lb	Rhubarb	900 g
6 oz	Granulated sugar	175 g
1	Egg yolk	1

Sift flour, pinch of salt and spices into a bowl. Rub in the butter till the mixture resembles fine breadcrumbs. Stir in the caster sugar and enough water to make a soft but not sticky dough. Knead lightly till smooth, then chill for 30 minutes.

Meanwhile, trim the rhubarb and cut into 1 inch (2.5 cm) lengths. Put into a bowl with all but 1 tbsp (15 ml) of the granulated sugar and mix well.

Preheat the oven to 400°F (200°C) Gas 6. Place a baking tray on the shelf just above the centre to heat up.

Roll out half the dough on a floured surface and use to line a 9 inch (23 cm) pie plate. Brush the edge with water. Pile the rhubarb into the pie in a dome shape. Roll out remaining dough and cover the pie, sealing and crimping the edges.

Beat the egg yolk and brush over top of pie. Place pie on hot baking tray and bake for 20 minutes. Reduce the temperature to 350°F (180°C) Gas 4 and bake for a further 25 minutes till crisp and golden.

Remove from the oven, sprinkle remaining sugar over and serve immediately with cream or pouring custard.

Irish lemon pudding

Overall timing 1 hour

Freezing Not suitable

To serve 4–6

4 oz	Butter	125 g
6 oz	Caster sugar	175 g
4	Eggs	4
1	Lemon	1
3 tbsp	Plain flour	3x15 ml
½ pint	Milk	300 ml
1 tbsp	Icing sugar	15 ml

Preheat the oven to 400°F (200°C) Gas 6.

Cream the butter and caster sugar in a bowl till light and fluffy. Separate the eggs and add the yolks to the creamed mixture. Beat well. Grate rind from lemon and squeeze out juice. Beat into the creamed mixture. Gradually stir in the flour, then the milk.

Beat egg whites till stiff, then carefully fold into mixture. Turn into a greased 7 inch (18 cm) soufflé dish and sift icing sugar over. Place dish in roasting tin containing 1 inch (2.5 cm) hot water. Bake for 40–50 minutes till the pudding has risen and the top is golden. Serve hot or cold.

Index